Dear Jim,
I pray this study
helps a you prepare the
Church to keep watch.
Richard

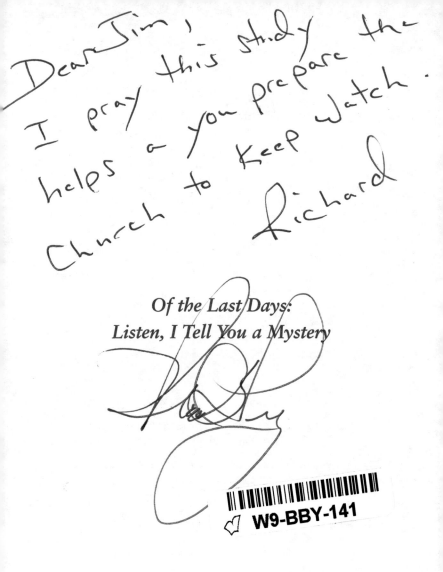

Of the Last Days:
Listen, I Tell You a Mystery

Of The Last Days:
LISTEN, I TELL YOU A MYSTERY

The truth concerning the return of Christ has become
hidden from much of the household of God

RICHARD H. PERRY

Belleville, Ontario, Canada

Of the Last Days: Listen, I Tell You a Mystery
Copyright © 2003, Richard H. Perry

All Scripture quotations, unless otherwise specified, are from *The Holy Bible, New International Version*. Copyright © 1973, 1978, 1984 International Bible Society. Used by permission of Zondervan Publishing House. All rights reserved. **Bold lettering** has been added in the text and scriptural references for emphasis.

National Library of Canada Cataloguing in Publication

Perry, Richard H. (Richard Hugo), 1947-
    Of the last days : listen, I tell you a mystery / Richard H. Perry.

Includes bibliographical references.
ISBN 1-55306-656-1.--ISBN 1-55306-595-6 (LSI ed.)

    1. Eschatology--Biblical teaching. I. Title.

BT821.3.P47 2003   236   C2003-903513-1

**For more information or
to order additional copies, please contact:**

Richard H. Perry
Web site:www.lastdaysmystery.info
Email:lastdaysmystery@yahoo.com

Guardian Books is an imprint of *Essence Publishing,* a Christian Book Publisher dedicated to furthering the work of Christ through the written word. For more information, contact:
20 Hanna Court, Belleville, Ontario, Canada K8P 5J2.
Phone: 1-800-238-6376 • Fax: (613) 962-3055.
E-mail: publishing@essencegroup.com
Internet: www.essencegroup.com

Dedicated to

The LORD, Jesus Christ, the God of your fathers—
the God of Abraham,
the God of Isaac
and the God of Jacob.

With gratitude to

Those who assisted in this, His work.

TABLE OF CONTENTS ———————————————

This glossary is provided to help the reader understand terms used in this study. With each term will be a list of synonyms followed by a definition. If a term is not found in the Bible, this will be stated in the definition.

ABOMINATION THAT CAUSES DESOLATION, THE

■ This event will happen when the Antichrist sets himself up in God's temple in Jerusalem, proclaiming himself to be God. It is prophesied to occur in the middle of Daniel's seventieth week—Daniel 9:27.

ANTICHRIST

■ 1 John 2:18)—the beast (Daniel 7:11; Revelation 13:3–5), the man of lawlessness (2 Thessalonians 2:3).

■ The world leader who will rise to power out of the fourth beast kingdom as prophesied in Daniel 7:23–24. He will confirm a covenant with Israel and then, after three and a half years, he will put a stop to the sacrifice and offering in the temple when he proclaims himself to be God. During the Great Tribulation, he will receive power from Satan as he deceives the world and attempts to destroy the people of God.

ARMAGEDDON

■ The place of the final battle where the kings of the earth and their armies are destroyed when Jesus Christ returns on the Day of the Lord (Revelation 16:16).

BABYLON THE GREAT, MYSTERY

■ Mystery Babylon.
■ A last days superpower which will hold a position of great influence over the world until destroyed by the Antichrist and the fourth beast kingdom (Revelation, chapters 17 and 18).

BEAST, THE

■ Antichrist, man of lawlessness.
■ The final leader of the fourth beast kingdom (Daniel 7:24). This incredibly successful world leader will receive power from Satan (Revelation 13:3), and attempt to destroy the people of God (Revelation 13:7).

BEAST KINGDOM, THE FOURTH

■ The fourth world kingdom which will rise to power during the last days and rule over the whole world. This kingdom will initially have ten kings, and then the Antichrist will arise among the ten and overthrow three of the kings. Then the kingdom will have seven heads and ten horns (Daniel 7:24).

BELIEVERS

■ Saints, chosen, elect, servants of God, followers of Christ, Christians, Church, Body of Christ, Bride of Christ.
■ Those who have placed their faith in Jesus Christ; those who have their names written in the book of life.

BOOK OF LIFE

■ God's record of all those who put their faith in Jesus Christ.

CHRIST

■ Messiah, Anointed One, Son of God.

■ The title of the anointed one of God; the Messiah who has come and will return to establish the Kingdom of God on earth.

DANIEL'S SEVENTIETH WEEK

■ The Tribulation

■ This non-biblical term refers to the last seven years of Daniel's "Seventy-sevens" prophecy. To date, 483 years of this 490-year prophecy have been completely fulfilled. One seven-year period is still outstanding and will be fulfilled in the last days (Daniel 9:24–27).

DAY OF THE LORD

■ Day of Wrath, Day of Salvation, Day of Redemption.

■ The day when Jesus Christ returns to gather His elect, punish the unbelieving world and establish the Kingdom of God on earth. The Day of the Lord is a very significant event in God's prophetic plan. It is referred to by name twenty-four times in Scripture and written about so often that the prophets abbreviated its name by referring to it as "*the day*" or "*that day.*" Several times in Scripture it is called "*the great and dreadful day*" because it will be both the day of deliverance and a day of judgment.

END OF THE AGE

■ The last day, Day of the Lord.

■ One of the terms Jesus used to refer to the time of the

harvest and His return, when He will gather His elect and judge the world.

FALSE PROPHET, THE

■ The second beast of Revelation 13 who comes out of the earth and deceives the whole world by performing miraculous signs, causing the inhabitants of the earth to worship the first beast. He and the first beast are thrown into the lake of fire at the end of the Great Tribulation.

HARVEST, THE

■ The First Resurrection, the resurrection of believers.
■ The gathering of the saints at the end of the age.

JUDGMENT SEAT OF CHRIST

■ The judgment of believers which will occur at the return of Jesus Christ. This is when the saints will receive their reward for what they have done in Christ (2 Corinthians 5:10).

KINGDOM OF GOD

■ Kingdom of Heaven, Kingdom.
■ The final earthly Kingdom, which will be ruled by Christ and His followers. There are other aspects to the Kingdom of God, such as the Kingdom of God in heaven and the Kingdom that exists in each believer. But, for the purposes of this study, whenever we refer to the Kingdom, it will be in reference to the coming earthly Kingdom of God.

LAST DAYS

■ End Times.
■ The period of time leading up to the return of Jesus Christ and the End of the Age.

Man of Lawlessness

■ Antichrist, the beast.

■ The leader of the fourth beast kingdom. This incredibly successful world leader will receive power from Satan and attempt to destroy the people of God.

Michael the Archangel

■ The archangel who protects the people of God (Daniel 12:1), and who in the last days will battle Satan and throw him to earth (Revelation 12:7).

Millennium

■ The non-biblical term for the thousand-year reign of Christ on earth (Revelation 20:2–7).

Rapture

■ A non-biblical term used to describe the catching up of living believers into the clouds to meet the Lord in the air, at the return of Christ (1 Thessalonians 4:17).

Rebellion, The

■ The Falling Away, the Apostasy.

■ The event Paul referred to in 2 Thessalonians 2:3 as marking the turning away from faith in Jesus Christ which will likely take place during the Great Tribulation.

Resurrection, First

■ The harvest, resurrection of believers.

■ The gathering and change that will take place in all believers at the return of Christ (Revelation 20:5).

Resurrection, Second

■ A non-biblical term for the raising of the rest of the dead at the end of the thousand-year reign of Christ on earth, Revelation 20:5.

Satan

■ The devil, the great dragon, that ancient serpent.
■ A powerful angel who rebelled against God and strives to rise to the throne of God by destroying the people and plans of God. He will be thrown to earth by Michael at the time of the abomination that causes desolation. Satan will give his power to the Antichrist during the Great Tribulation until he is captured and bound in the Abyss for a thousand years.

Scripture

■ Bible, Word, Word of God, Word of Truth, Gospel.
■ The holy, written and infallible Word of God.

Second Coming

■ Second Advent, return of Christ.
■ A non-biblical term for the return of Jesus Christ from heaven to earth.

Temple, The

■ House of God.
■ The structure called the "House of God" and the place of Jewish worship in Jerusalem. Solomon built the first temple. The second temple was rebuilt during the time of Nehemiah, and Herod restored it to a state of grandeur during the time of Christ's First Advent. The second temple was completely destroyed in A.D. 70, just as Jesus prophesied. There will be a third temple built sometime in the future.

TRIBULATION, THE

■ Daniel's Seventieth Week.

■ A non-biblical term which refers to the seven-year period at the end of the age, as prophesied in Daniel 9:27.

TRUMPET, THE LAST

■ The seventh trumpet of Revelation 11:15, which will signal the resurrection of the living and the dead in Christ (1 Corinthians 15:51,52).

TRIBULATION, THE GREAT

■ Time of Jacob's Trouble.

■ The three-and-a-half-year period of unparalleled persecution and suffering of God's people brought on by Satan through the Antichrist and False Prophet. This is the most documented period of time recorded in Scripture, being referred to as: forty-two months, 1,260 days, and a time, times and half a time. This period begins with the *abomination that causes desolation* and ends with the return of Christ at the end of the age (Matthew 24:21).

WHITE THRONE JUDGMENT, THE GREAT

■ The final judgment which will take place after the thousand-year earthly reign of Christ. The White Throne Judgment appears to be the judgment of everyone who did not take part in the First Resurrection (Revelation 20:11).

WEDDING BANQUET, THE

■ The wedding feast, the wedding supper.

■ The celebration of the union between Jesus Christ and the Bride of Christ (all true believers). It will take place on Mount Zion in Jerusalem, as described in Isaiah 25:6–8.

Word of Truth

■ Bible, Scripture, Word, Gospel, Word of God.
■ The holy, written and infallible Word of God.

Wrath of God

■ Day of the Lord.
■ God's judgment and punishment on the unbelieving and disobedient world, which will be poured out on the Day of the Lord.

As a child I attended a small-town church where I was introduced to stories of the Old Testament and the life of Christ. When I left home to attend college I left the church as well, attending only during the holidays. However, while I was in college, my dad was born again, and both he and my mom began to pray that I would come to know Christ.

Eight years later, while I was visiting my parents one weekend, I was reading the international news and giving my Mom a prognosis of where the world was headed. She looked up from what she was doing and said, "That's interesting; many Christians believe that is what is predicted in the Bible's Book of Revelation." Out of curiosity, I dug out my Bible. As I read through Revelation, I became intrigued by what was written, but many of the things described seemed impossible to understand. So, I purchased a couple of books written about the prophecies of Revelation. While the authors used different approaches, they both indicated that the keys to understanding the Book of Revelation were contained in the rest of the Bible.

Over the next four months I read through the entire Bible. Somewhere in the epistles of the New Testament I realized that, by God's perfect standard, I was in serious trouble with the way I was living my life. But fortunately I also realized there was a solution and I needed what only Christ could offer. I accepted Him for who He claimed to be and asked Him into my life as my Lord and my God. He promised to help me turn from my ways and follow Him.

For over twenty years, the Lord has been leading and teaching me about Himself and His plans. At times in our relationship, He has had my undivided attention, while at other times I wandered aimlessly, distracted with the cares of life. However, He has never allowed me to get very far from Him before He gives a gentle tug or a stronger form of encouragement, calling me to listen and obey.

Several years ago, He led me to Central America, with Habitat for Humanity International. During the nearly six years I was there, He taught me some of the most amazing things about Himself. I had the chance to see Him in ways that would not have been possible had I been in my own culture. One lesson He began to teach me, and which I am still learning today, is captured in Proverbs:

> *Trust in the LORD with all your heart and lean not on your own understanding; in all your ways acknowledge him, and he will make your paths straight* (Proverbs 3:5,6).

During these last several years that I have been back in the United States, God has revealed to me that many churches in the United States suffer from what can only be called a **Famine for the Word of God**. This condition for the coming days was prophesied in both the Old and New Testaments.

> *The days are coming, declares the Sovereign LORD, when I will send a famine through the land—not a*

famine of food or a thirst for water, but a famine of hearing the words of the LORD. *Men will stagger from sea to sea and wander from north to east, searching for the word of the* LORD, *but they will not find it* (Amos 8:11,12).

For the time will come when men will not put up with sound doctrine. Instead, to suit their own desires, they will gather around them a great number of teachers to say what their itching ears want to hear (2 Timothy 4:3).

The **Famine for the Word of God** is contributing to many problems in churches and communities. It is not that the Word of God is not available. We have more Bibles and biblical resources today than at any time in history. The problem comes because the Word of God is being distorted and people are not studying their Bibles. Since people are not reading the Word of God, they are unfamiliar with the commandments of Christ, which are needed to guide their lives. Without knowledge of the Word, they only have the rules of this world by which to conduct themselves. Because of this condition, many who attend church have no saltiness or light. But the true followers of Jesus Christ are always "the salt of the earth" and "the light of the world."

You are the salt of the earth. But if the salt loses its saltiness, how can it be made salty again? It is no longer good for anything, except to be thrown out and trampled by men. You are the light of the world. A city on a hill cannot be hidden (Matthew 5:13,14).

For many years, as I have studied the Bible, I have encountered differences between what is written in Scripture and what is being taught in churches and written in Christian books. These differences vary from individual to individual and denomination to denomination, but on no doctrinal position is the difference greater than on the return of Christ.

As I have searched the Word of Truth over the years, the Holy Spirit has provided many insights into the last days. The more familiar with Scripture I became, the more I could see the connections between prophecies. As I examined Scripture, a comprehensive picture developed of what God has foretold about the future.

The basic elements of the end times are clear and easy to understand. The revelation provided is more than sufficient to show us how to recognize the signs of the times. The last days are not hard to find in the Scripture, with about an eighth of the Bible written on the topic. It is clearly God's desire that we read and understand His Word about what is ahead. As a matter of fact, of the hundreds of books I have read on the topic of the last days, there is none easier to understand than the Bible itself. However, as a dear brother once told me, "It's all right there in the Word, you just have to read it a few hundred times." What he said is true. While the Bible contains the truth, we are the ones that have to do the work of faithfully seeking it out. God instructs us to seek, and He assures us we will find. *"So I say to you: Ask and it will be given to you; seek and you will find; knock and the door will be opened to you"* (Luke 11:9).

However, today most people are pursuing an eschatology developed by man and not found in the Word of God. In my early years of Bible study, I thought that the differences I saw were due to my lack of knowledge. I listened intently to what was being taught and it all sounded reasonable to my untrained ears. Teachers made convincing cases for their positions, quoting liberally from Scripture. I was naïvely comfortable, feeling that I was receiving sound biblical teaching. However, the more I studied and compared what was being taught with what was written in the Word, the more I became convinced that there were significant and serious differences.

As I discussed these differences with other Christians, I encountered a variety of reactions. Some were confused and others frustrated. However, the great majority were ambivalent and did not seem to think the topic was important. Most would brush off attempted discussions with humor, saying things like, "I'm a Pan-Tribulationist," or "I'm a Pan-Millennialist—I believe it will all pan out in the end," or they would say, "As long as you know Jesus, it's not important."

The pastors and teachers I questioned about these differences would almost always indicate they were teaching what they were taught. When I asked them to show me how they arrived at their conclusions, they would refer me to some book on the topic—but not the Bible. I have yet to have a pastor or teacher take me through Scripture to support a doctrinal position on the return of Christ. One of the most common responses I have heard goes something like this: "Smarter people than I have studied these things and cannot agree, so what chance do I have?" While this sounds like a legitimate excuse, *it is not.*

When pastors or Bible teachers claim to be unable to understand the Bible—while Scripture says they can—that is actually a form of unbelief. Unbelief poses a serious problem for the church today. You can imagine what this communicates to the household of God under the care of these leaders, which is why the Lord warns those who claim to be teachers of the Word: "*Not many of you should presume to be teachers, my brothers, because you know that we who teach will be judged more strictly*" (James 3:1).

Because pastors and Bible teachers believe themselves unable to understand the truth about the return of Christ, two serious problems have developed in the Body of Christ. **First, many pastors and teachers have avoided teaching and preaching on the return of Christ and about the last days**. This deprives the church of critically important teachings from the Word of God, leaving the household of God ignorant and uninformed of what is coming on the world. For the Bible reveals with great certainty that, at some time in the future, the whole world will find itself in the middle of the last days. The question is, when the last days come upon the world, will the household of God be informed and prepared?

> *Who then is the faithful and wise servant, whom the master has put in charge of the servants in his household to give them their food at the proper time? It will be good for that servant whose master finds him doing so when he returns* (Matthew 24:45,46).

This brings us to another question: when is the proper time to teach the household of God about the return of Christ and the last days? Of course, the Scripture has the answer to this timely question. In the Great Commission to the Church, in Matthew 28:18–20, Jesus gave us clear marching orders. As we go about the process of making disciples, we are to teach them to obey everything that Christ commanded. Since one of Jesus' major teachings was regarding His return and the coming Kingdom, that must also be part of what is taught in the household of God as we go about making disciples. Therefore, the Church must always be teaching about the return of Christ and the end of the age.

Second, many pastors and teachers have by default taught the teachings of man. Because many feel unable to determine the truth for themselves, they have turned to the teachings of man. This is a serious problem when their teachings are not tested against the Word of God. Unfortunately, most people in the household of God do not study the Word, nor do they test what they hear against the Word. This leaves the teachings of man unchecked and the people uninformed and ignorant as to the truth regarding the return of Christ.

These problems have either been orchestrated by Satan or have played nicely into his hands. The absence of correct biblical teaching on the last days and the unchecked teachings of man have ushered division, confusion and deception into the Church. Shouldn't someone say, **Let's find unity and truth regarding the Lord's return before it's too late?** We know from the Bible that God has called us to guard the doctrine of the gospel and He also deeply desires that we be in unity under His Lordship. *"Watch your life and doctrine closely. Persevere in them, because if you do, you will save both yourself and your hearers"* (1 Timothy 4:16).

> *He must hold firmly to the trustworthy message as it has been taught, so that he can encourage others by sound doctrine and refute those who oppose it* (Titus 1:9).

> *May they be brought to complete unity to let the world know that you sent me and have loved them even as you have loved me* (John 17:23).

This brings us to the point of this study. For the past several years, the Lord has impressed two things upon me. **First, all of His Word is critically important,** meaning all of His Word carries eternal significance that affects the eternal destiny of all people. **Second, He wants His Church to know the truth about His return.** He wants the Church to be spiritually prepared, waiting, watching and ready for what lies ahead.

In 2001, the Lord led me to teach an end times Bible study in our local community. During that time, the Lord woke me early one morning and pressed me to pray about the study. As I was praying, He gave me two messages. The first was an answer to a question I had been asking Him for months: how important are the biblical prophecies regarding the return of Christ? He gave me the same answer that He had given Israel's religious leaders almost 2,000 years ago:

> As he approached Jerusalem and saw the city, he wept over it and said, "If you, even you, had only known on this day what would bring you peace— but now it is hidden from your eyes. The days will come upon you when your enemies will build an embankment against you and encircle you and hem you in on every side. They will dash you to the ground, you and the children within your walls. They will not leave one stone on another, **because you did not recognize the time of God's coming to you**" (Luke 19:41–44).

I received this message a couple months after 9/11/2001, so the impact of such a tremendous loss of life was still fresh upon my mind. Jesus said that **because** the Jewish leaders did not recognize the timing of His first coming, their city would be destroyed and their people slaughtered. His prophecy was literally fulfilled thirty-eight years later, when the armies of the Roman general Titus slaughtered over one million Jews and destroyed Jerusalem. My understanding of His message is this: His prophecies are a matter of life and death for the Church and the eternal destiny of many.

The second message was, "See Dr. Schaefer." The only Dr. Schaefer I was aware of is a professor of chemistry at the University of Georgia. He has won awards for academic excellence and is known for his leadership in the University's Christian Faculty Forum. A couple of years previously, my wife and I had attended a lecture he gave called "The Ten Questions Intellectuals Ask About Christianity."

I attempted to contact Dr. Schaefer later that morning. When I reached his secretary, she asked what the call was about. At first I told her that I was not sure, but then I explained to her how the Lord had prompted me to see Dr. Schaefer. She said she would give him the message. Later that day, Dr. Schaefer returned my call and I related to him what had happened. Although he was very busy, he said we should meet.

During our meeting I explained what the Lord had placed on my heart. He indicated that he had taught through the Book of Revelation several times and he questioned me on the topic. We continued our discussion for about an hour, and, as we were closing, I thanked him for the opportunity to meet and talk. Then I said, "I don't know why the Lord put us together, but I appreciate the time you have given me." He paused, looked at me and said, "I believe you are supposed to write a book." I received his message as direction from the Lord to write this book of the last days.

I believe the Lord would have me write this as a study of the Bible revealing what is written in Scripture regarding the last days and the return of Christ. It is my desire to follow carefully the biblical instructions for interpreting the Word of God. In the next chapter I will outline the rules God has given for correctly handling the Word of Truth. It is my intention to allow Scripture to interpret Scripture, and to compare related passages, so that you can see what God has revealed about the return of Christ.

May the Lord bless and guide this, His work; and may we not turn to the left or to the right as we attempt to determine the truth about the return of Christ and the end of the age.

CHAPTER ONE

Correctly Handling the Word of Truth

Before we begin this study of the last days and the return of Christ, we need to understand how God says to interpret His Word. The Bible indicates there are correct ways to handle the Word of Truth. This means there are also incorrect ways. One reason there are many different interpretations of the end times is that people do not follow the instructions God has given for the interpretation of His Word.

*Do your best to present yourself to God as one approved, a workman who does not need to be ashamed and who **correctly handles the word of truth** (2 Timothy 2:15).*

Paul's words to Timothy reveal an interesting truth for handling the Word of Truth—it requires *work*. A workman applies his best effort to his trade on a regular basis.

Interpreting the Bible correctly is not an accident; it is a deliberate effort, and the result of ongoing application and study. Since Paul expected Timothy to be a workman in this effort, we should expect no different requirement for us today.

> Do not let this Book of the Law depart from your mouth; meditate on it day and night, so that you may be careful to do everything written in it. Then you will be prosperous and successful (Joshua 1:8).

The work of interpreting the Word of God is important work. It requires continuous study and meditation. It should become a part of our lifestyle. This type of life builds up and transforms, leading to maturity in Christ. However, just as correctly handling the Word leads to maturity, incorrectly handling the Word leads to false teaching, deception and ultimately destruction.

"Do not add to his words, or he [God] will rebuke you and prove you a liar" (Proverbs 30:6). No matter how sure you are about what God meant by a particular verse, it is very dangerous to add your opinion to His divine wisdom. Few things could be worse than the rebuke of God, and nothing could be worse than being proved a liar by God. Not only does the incorrect use of the Word of God have serious consequences for the careless teacher, it can also be detrimental for others:

> [M]y people are destroyed from lack of knowledge. Because you have rejected knowledge, I also reject you as my priests; because you have ignored the law of your God, I also will ignore your children (Hosea 4:6).

It is no wonder God gives such grave warnings against incorrectly handling His Word, since lives are at stake. In the closing words of the Book of Revelation, the Lord issues one of the most direct warnings of the entire Bible:

> *I warn everyone who hears the words of the prophecy of this book: If anyone adds anything to them, God will add to him the plagues described in this book. And if anyone takes words away from this book of prophecy, God will take away from him his share in the tree of life and in the holy city, which are described in this book* (Revelation 22:18,19).

This same warning was first issued in the Old Testament when God opened the law to Israel: "*Do not add to what I command you and do not subtract from it, but keep the commands of the* LORD *your God that I give you*" (Deuteronomy 4:2).

■ THE BIBLE IS TO BE READ AND UNDERSTOOD

God inspired His Word to reveal Himself, His purposes and His plans. The Bible is a comprehensive communication from God to man. The Bible itself answers the questions it raises, which is why we say Scripture interprets Scripture. God did not prepare His Word to be confusing or misleading. He says what He means and He means what He says. "*For we do not write you anything you cannot read or understand*" (2 Corinthians 1:13).

The gospel of Christ is meant for everyone. In that spirit, Paul's letters to the Corinthians were written to be read to the whole body of believers, not just the pastors and teachers. It was customary for these letters to be copied and distributed to other bodies of believers. In fact, people who come to the Word like little children will be more inclined to understand the Word than those who think they already know something. "*Where is the wise man? Where is the scholar? Where is the philosopher of this age? Has not God made foolish the wisdom of the world?* (1 Corinthians 1:20).

> *And he said: 'I tell you the truth, unless you change and become like little children, you will never enter the kingdom of heaven. Therefore, whoever humbles himself like this child is the greatest in the kingdom of heaven'* (Matthew 18:3,4).

God meant His Word to be understood. The gospel of Jesus Christ and all the epistles that make up the New Testament were written in the Greek language used by the common people of the day.

However, there are two requirements for being able to understand the Word of God:

1. We must have the Holy Spirit.

"The Holy Spirit, whom the Father will send in my name, will teach you all things and will remind you of everything I have said to you" (John 14:26). The Bible teaches that a man without the Spirit cannot understand spiritual truths. It is very important as we study spiritual truth that we seek the guidance of the Holy Spirit.

> *This is what we speak, not in words taught us by human wisdom but in words taught by the Spirit, expressing spiritual truths in spiritual words. The man without the Spirit does not accept the things that come from the Spirit of God, for they are foolishness to him, and he cannot understand them, because they are spiritually discerned* (1 Corinthians 2:13,14).

2. We must seek the Truth.

Scripture also reveals that the Truth is revealed to those

that seek it with a pure heart. In other words, Scripture is revealed to those who are not encumbered by ulterior motives. If you are studying the Word to prove your opinion or to support your own personal theology, you will not find Truth. The Truth of the Word is revealed to those who honestly want to know it. These passages indicate that if we do not approach the Word with a mind open to the Truth of God, we may not be able to receive it: "*The LORD is near to all who call on him, to all who call on him in truth*" (Psalm 145:18); "*And he said: 'I tell you the truth, unless you change and become like little children, you will never enter the kingdom of heaven'*" (Matthew 18:3). "*The unfolding of your words gives light; it gives understanding to the simple*" (Psalm 119:130).

Our pride, our education, our positions, our accomplishments and even our ideas can frustrate the pursuit of truth.

> *At that time Jesus said, "I praise you, Father, Lord of heaven and earth, because you have hidden these things from the wise and learned, and revealed them to little children"* (Matthew 11:25).

> *For it is written: 'I will destroy the wisdom of the wise; the intelligence of the intelligent I will frustrate.' Where is the wise man? Where is the scholar? Where is the philosopher of this age? Has not God made foolish the wisdom of the world?* (1 Corinthians 1:19,20).

Before we go any further, ask the Holy Spirit to reveal any ulterior motives and any biases that may hinder your pursuit of truth.

There will be false teachers among you

One vital reason to handle the Word of Truth correctly is to defend against false doctrines and false teachers. These teachers and doctrines are not just cults and false religions. They find their way into Christian churches that are not defended against them. Scripture indicates deception will increase in the household of God until there will be little truth remaining. Jesus stated the deception would be so strong that even the elect would be deceived, if that were possible: *"many false prophets will appear and deceive many people"* (Matthew 24:11).

> *But there were also false prophets among the people, just as **there will be false teachers among you**. They will secretly introduce destructive heresies, even denying the sovereign Lord who bought them— bringing swift destruction on themselves* (2 Peter 2:1).

> *For the time will come when men will not put up with sound doctrine. Instead, to suit their own desires, they will gather around them a great number of teachers to say what their itching ears want to hear. They will turn their ears away from the truth and turn aside to myths* (2 Timothy 4:3,4).

> *For false Christs and false prophets will appear and perform great signs and miracles to deceive even the elect—if that were possible. See, I have told you ahead of time* (Matthew 24:24,25).

The extent to which false doctrine is manifest today is indeed frightening. This is particularly true regarding much of what we hear about the return of Jesus Christ. The purpose of this book is not to investigate false teachings.

However, our understanding of the doctrine of the return of Christ and the resurrection of believers will certainly help reveal what is false about the popular teachings of our day.

Since there are many false teachers and there is much deception in the household of God, it will be helpful for us to know the characteristics of those who proclaim the Word falsely. Thankfully, God revealed a great deal about false prophets in the Old Testament. He says, in Jeremiah and Ezekiel:

> This is what the LORD Almighty says: "Do not listen to what the prophets are prophesying to you; **they fill you with false hopes**. They speak visions from their own minds, not from the mouth of the LORD. They keep saying to those who despise me, 'The LORD says: You will have peace.' And to all who follow the stubbornness of their hearts they say, 'No harm will come to you.' But which of them has stood in the council of the LORD to see or to hear his word? …"Therefore," declares the LORD, "I am against the prophets who steal from one another words supposedly from me (Jeremiah 23:16–30).

> The word of the LORD came to me: "Son of man, prophesy against the prophets of Israel who are now prophesying. Say to those who prophesy out of their own imagination: 'Hear the word of the LORD! This is what the Sovereign LORD says: Woe to the foolish prophets who follow their own spirit and have seen nothing! …Their visions are false and their divinations a lie. They say, 'The LORD declares,' when the LORD has not sent them; yet they expect their words to be fulfilled (Ezekiel 13:1–6).

Characteristics of false prophets:

1. They speak from their own imaginations.
2. They do not have a word from God.
3. They prophesy false hope—"No harm will come to you."
4. They take words from one another supposedly from God.
5. They expect their words to be fulfilled.

Fortunately, we have the complete revelation of God's Word in Scripture and are able to test everything against the Word to see if what we are told is true.

■ BASICS FOR CORRECTLY HANDLING THE WORD OF TRUTH

The following outline provides the biblical instructions we will need to correctly handle the Word of Truth.

1. The Bible is the Word of Truth.

Both the Old and New Testaments have stood the test of time as the uniquely inspired Word of God. For the seeker of Truth, the Bible has revealed itself as the completely credible and authoritative communication from the Creator. *"Your word, O LORD, is eternal; it stands firm in the heavens"* (Psalms 119:89); *"Righteous are you, O LORD, and your laws are right. The statutes you have laid down are righteous; they are fully trustworthy"* (Psalm 119:137,138); *"All Scripture is God-breathed and is useful for teaching, rebuking, correcting and training in righteousness"* (2 Timothy 3:16).

> *Above all, you must understand that no prophecy of Scripture came about by the prophet's own interpretation. For prophecy never had its origin in the will of man, but men spoke from God as they were carried along by the Holy Spirit* (2 Peter 1:20,21).

2. What is prophesied will happen.

One of the distinguishing characteristics of the Holy Bible is that it makes clear predictions concerning what will happen in the future. To date, approximately half of the Bible's prophecies have been fulfilled just as they were foretold. *"Everything must be fulfilled that is written about me in the Law of Moses, the Prophets and the Psalms"* (Luke 24:44).

> *I tell you the truth, until heaven and earth disappear, not the smallest letter, not the least stroke of a pen, will by any means disappear from the Law until everything is accomplished* (Matthew 5:18).

One of the most amazing examples of fulfilled biblical prophecy occurred when Jesus Christ made His triumphal ride into Jerusalem. This took place on the exact day God said it would, through the prophet Daniel, over 600 years prior to the event. We will examine this prophecy in more detail when we study Daniel's prophecies.

> *Know and understand this: From the issuing of the decree to restore and rebuild Jerusalem until the Anointed One, the ruler, comes, there will be seven 'sevens,' and sixty-two 'sevens'* (Daniel 9:25).

The "*sevens*" referred to are periods of years. One "*seven*" equals seven years, therefore "*seven sevens*" and "*sixty-two sevens*" totals sixty-nine sevens. This equals 483 years, the exact span of time from Artaxerxes' decree to Christ's triumphal entry into Jerusalem. This remarkable prophecy is just one of hundreds which have already been fulfilled.

The prophets of God whom we encounter in Scripture were established by the standard set forth in Deuteronomy 18:22. Their prophecies have been (or will be) fulfilled just as they are written. "*If what a prophet proclaims in the name of the* LORD *does not take place or come true, that is a message the* LORD *has not spoken*" (Deuteronomy 18:22).

To date, about half of their prophecies have been fulfilled, which means the other half will be fulfilled sometime in the future. The majority of these unfulfilled prophecies relate to the return of Jesus Christ and the coming Kingdom of God on earth.

3. We can understand the Truth.

As we have already discussed, God tells us we can read and understand the Word of Truth. He has not made it difficult or complicated. To the contrary, He has made it so straightforward that He tells us that we must come to it as little children. "*For we do not write you anything you cannot read or understand*" (2 Corinthians 1:13); "*Ask and it will be given to you; seek and you will find; knock and the door will be opened to you*" (Matthew 7:7).

The Lord also tells us that the Holy Spirit will guide and teach us all things to ensure that we understand the truth of the Gospel:

> *But the Counselor, the Holy Spirit, whom the Father will send in my name, will teach you all things and will remind you of everything I have said to you* (John 14:26).

> *But when he, the Spirit of truth, comes, he will guide you into all truth. He will not speak on his own; he will speak only what he hears, and he will tell you what is yet to come* (John 16:13).

4. Don't add to or take away from the Word.

Because God desires that we know and understand the

Truth, He has provided clear instructions so we will know how to read and understand the Word of Truth. These instructions reveal to us that we are not to go beyond what He has said. These instructions protect us from the notion that the Bible does not mean what it says or that it means something that it does *not* state. Read these examples of biblical instruction and see for yourself how emphatic the Lord is regarding His Word: "*Do not add to what I command you and do not subtract from it, but keep the commands of the* LORD *your God that I give you* (Deuteronomy 4:2); "*See that you do all I command you; do not add to it or take away from it*" (Deuteronomy 12:32); "*Every word of God is flawless; he is a shield to those who take refuge in him. Do not add to his words, or he will rebuke you and prove you a liar*" (Proverbs 30:5,6).

> *Remember your Creator in the days of your youth, before the days of trouble come... before the sun and the light and the moon and the stars grow dark.... The Teacher searched to find just the right words, and what he wrote was upright and true....* **Be warned, my son, of anything in addition to them** (Ecclesiastes 12:1–12).

> *Therefore judge nothing before the appointed time; wait till the Lord comes. He will bring to light what is hidden in darkness and will expose the motives of men's hearts. ...* **'***Do not go beyond what is written.***'** *Then you will not take pride in one man over against another* (I Corinthians 4:5,6).

> *I warn everyone who hears the words of the prophecy of this book: If anyone adds anything to them, God will add to him the plagues described in*

this book. And if anyone takes words away from this book of prophecy, God will take away from him his share in the tree of life and in the holy city, which are described in this book (Revelation 22:18,19).

God used over forty writers spanning 1,500 years to say exactly what He meant. He does not need editors and commentators to improve upon what He said. Implicit in these instructions is the warning not to change anything that has been written. Changing a word of Scripture certainly violates the instructions against taking away from and adding to His Word.

Jesus' ministry demonstrates the reverence we are to have for Scripture. Over and over He uses the phase, *"it is written,"* indicating we are to accept by faith what is written in the Word of God. Jesus makes other statements which further instruct us how to read and understand the Bible. For example, Jesus says, *"the Scriptures... say it must happen in this way"* (Matthew 26:54). Everything Jesus teaches about the Word indicates He means what He says and says what He means. Do you believe it?

A very serious error in handling the Word of God is the interpretation of Scripture using only metaphors and allegories. An allegory is the description of one thing under the image of another.[1] Scripture is, of course, replete with allegory and metaphors, which are vitally important for a rich and full understanding of the gospel. However, allegories and metaphors foundational to doctrine are always explained in the Word. For example, in the Book of Revelation, Jesus Christ is referred to as *"the Lamb"* almost thirty times. This metaphor for Jesus Christ is important to a proper understanding of Revelation. So, how can we be sure the *"the Lamb"* is Jesus Christ? Because, Scripture states that *"the Lamb"* is Jesus: *"The next day John saw Jesus coming toward him and said, 'Look, the Lamb of God, who takes away the sin of the world!'"* (John 1:29).

As we can see, symbolism that is part of doctrinal teachings will always be explained by the Word. Any system of theology based only on allegory and metaphor and without the support of clear statements of Scripture is bankrupt. Such a theology will be prone to error and deception, leading its followers to destruction. For example, if someone says something written in Scripture actually means something else, they must have Scripture which clearly confirms their position or they are relying on their own interpretation. All doctrine must be based on the clear statements in the Word of God. All else is sinking sand.

5. Use the whole counsel of God.

We cannot accept an interpretation of Scripture as true if it is not in agreement with the whole of Scripture. There are no contradictions or inconsistencies in God's Holy Word. *"God is not a man, that he should lie, nor a son of man, that he should change his mind. Does he speak and then not act? Does he promise and not fulfill?"* (Numbers 23:19).

Also, remember that Scripture taken out of context ceases to be Scripture. *"All* [the sum of] *your words are true; all* [the sum of] *your righteous laws are eternal"* (Psalms 119:160); *"Jesus answered, 'It is written: Man does not live on bread alone, but on every word that comes from the mouth of God'"* (Matthew 4:4).

It is also important to understand that **until we have the full gospel of Jesus Christ, we do not have the true gospel.** A partial gospel is no gospel at all. That is why it was important to the apostle Paul that he proclaimed the whole gospel as recorded in Acts 20:27: *"For I have not hesitated to proclaim to you the whole will of God"* (Acts 20:27). The gospel of Jesus Christ includes the complete Scripture from Genesis through Revelation.

6. *Test everything to see if it is true.*

Now that we know how to read and understand the Word of Truth, we need to avoid getting carried away by every teaching that sounds good. Scripture instructs us how to keep ourselves from being deceived. *"Test everything. Hold on to the good"* (1 Thessalonians 5:21).

> *Now the Bereans were of more noble character than the Thessalonians, for they received the message with great eagerness and **examined the Scriptures every day to see if what Paul said was true** (Acts 17:11).*

> *Dear friends, do not believe every spirit, but **test the spirits** to see whether they are from God, **because many false prophets have gone out into the world** (1 John 4:1).*

Because many false teachers are already among us and there is deception in the household of God, we are told to test everything to see if what we hear is true. God has even given us three tests to use:

> *For if someone comes to you and preaches a Jesus other than the Jesus we preached, or if you receive a different spirit from the one you received, or a different gospel from the one you accepted, you put up with it easily enough (2 Corinthians 11:4).*

These are the three tests:

1. Is the Jesus presented the one of the gospel?

2. Is the Spirit consistent with the one we received?
3. Is the gospel consistent with what is written in Scripture?

First, we are to determine if the Jesus Christ presented is the one of the gospel. For example, Jesus said, *"I told you that you would die in your sins; if you do not believe that I am the one I claim to be, you will indeed die in your sins"* (John 8:24). Over and over in the Gospels, Jesus claims to be and proves that He is God. His Jewish audience was very aware that He was claiming deity for Himself. They said, *"We are not stoning you for any of these... but for blasphemy, because you, a mere man, claim to be God"* (John 10:33). So, the first test concerns the deity of Christ. Two well-known groups today deny that Jesus is God: Jehovah's Witnesses and the Church of the Latter Day Saints. The Jehovah's Witnesses believe that Jesus is the archangel Michael, and the Mormon Church believes that Jesus is *a* god, not *the* one and only Almighty God.

Second, we are to test the Spirit. The Spirit must be consistent with the Spirit of God we received. For example, if a spirit promises that we will not face tribulation, distress or persecution—that would be a deceptive spirit. The Spirit of God consistently reveals that we will face tribulation and persecution. Hear what the Spirit says: *"Therefore, brothers, in all our distress and persecution we were encouraged about you because of your faith"* (1 Thessalonians 3:7); *"Remember the words I spoke to you: 'No servant is greater than his master.' If they persecuted me, they will persecute you also"* (John 15:20).

Third and finally, we are to determine whether or not what we hear is consistent with what is written in Scripture. For example, if someone says Jesus will come and gather His Church before the Tribulation, we are to test it against the Word of Truth. When we find that Jesus says,

> *Immediately after the [tribulation] distress of those days... the Son of Man will appear in the sky, ... And he will send his angels with a loud trumpet call, and they will gather his elect...* (Matthew 24:29–31),

we are to believe it.

As we can see, there is ample reason to remain spiritually alert against false teaching and deception even in the household of God. If we stay spiritually alert, we protect ourselves against deception.

■ OUR STUDY GUIDELINES

Therefore, in keeping with the instructions and warnings provided by the Word of God, we will use the following guidelines to approach our study.

1. We will take our understanding of prophecy from the context, interpreting the words at face value using their normal and literal meaning. As we interpret Scripture, we will also take into consideration the use of:

   • Figures of speech, for example, "white as snow."
   • Metaphors such as "the Lamb," "the dragon."
   • Amplifications—restatements used to amplify an idea.
   • Allegories.

2. We will interpret prophecies concerning the future in a manner consistent with the prophecies that have already been fulfilled.

3. We will seek to let Scripture interpret Scripture. This means that, when seeking to answer questions raised by Scripture, our first recourse will be to examine Scripture itself for the answer. We will look for related Scriptures until we have the most complete picture.

4. We will obediently follow all biblical instructions
    regarding the interpretation of the Word of God, such as:

    a) Trust the Word of God.
    b) Do not add to or take away from the Word.
    c) Do not go beyond what is written.
    d) Use the whole Word.
    e) Test everything against the Word.

Therefore, "*To the law and to the testimony! If they do
not speak according to this word, they have no light of
Dawn*" (Isaiah 8:29).

Now, guided by the Holy Spirit and these biblical
instructions, let us begin our search of the Holy Scripture to
see what the Bible says regarding the last days and the
return of Jesus Christ.

CHAPTER TWO

According to the Lord's Own Word

> *According to the Lord's own word,*
> *we tell you that we who are still alive,*
> *who are left till the coming of the Lord,*
> *will certainly not precede those who have*
> *fallen asleep* (1 Thessalonians 4:15).

There can hardly be a better place to begin our study of the return of Christ and the end of the age than by examining what Jesus Christ has to say. According to the Old Testament, the Messiah will come to establish the Kingdom of God on earth. He will reign from the throne of David, in Jerusalem. From the very beginning of Jesus' ministry, He taught about the coming Kingdom and the end of the age. His most comprehensive teaching on the topic is called the Olivet Discourse, which is recorded in the first three Gospels of the New Testament (Matthew, Mark and Luke). Jesus gave the Olivet Discourse in response to the disciples' inquiry regarding His return. However, He had already taught extensively about the end of the age and the coming Kingdom of God. Therefore, before we go to the Olivet Discourse, we will first review Jesus' earlier teachings.

■ THERE WILL BE TWO AGES

During Jesus' ministry, He referred to two ages—this present age in which we now live, and a second age which is to come in the future. Below are some of His teachings about the two ages:

> *Anyone who speaks a word against the Son of Man will be forgiven, but anyone who speaks against the Holy Spirit will not be forgiven, either in this age or in the age to come* (Matthew 12:32).

> *'I tell you the truth,' Jesus said to them, 'no one who has left home or wife or brothers or parents or children for the sake of the kingdom of God will fail to receive many times as much in this age and, in the age to come, eternal life'* (Luke 18:29,30).

> *Jesus replied, 'The people of this age marry and are given in marriage. But those who are considered worthy of taking part in that age and in the resurrection from the dead will neither marry nor be given in marriage, and they can no longer die; for they are like the angels. They are God's children, since they are children of the resurrection'* (Luke 20:34–36).

The present age, the one in which we now live, most likely began in the Garden of Eden when Adam and Eve sinned by disobeying God. In contrast to the present age, Jesus teaches about an age of righteousness that will come after the present age. The age to come will begin when Christ establishes the Kingdom of God on earth. That is the age all believers are waiting for. In Luke 20:34, Jesus tells us that those worthy to take part in *"that age"* will be called children of the resurrection.

As we can see, Jesus refers to only two ages, *"this age"* and the *"age to come."* Therefore, we should not believe those who say there are many ages.

■ THE COMING KINGDOM OF GOD

The Parable of the Wheat and Tares is one of several parables Jesus employs to tell us about the coming Kingdom of God. The parable is about a man who sowed good seed in his field, but when the crop sprouted it was discovered that someone had planted bad seed among the good. The servants asked if they should weed out the bad from the good. The master told the servants to let both grow together until the *"harvest"* and then the good wheat would be gathered into the barn and the tares burned. The Parable of the Wheat and Tares provides insight into how and when the coming Kingdom of God will come.

On this occasion, His disciples asked Jesus for an explanation of the Parable of the Wheat and Tares. This is what He said—

*The one who sowed the good seed is the Son of Man. The field is the world, and the good seed stands for the sons of the kingdom. The weeds are the sons of the evil one, and the enemy who sows them is the devil. **The harvest is the end of the age, and the harvesters are angels.** As the weeds are pulled up and burned in the fire, so it will be at the end of the age. The Son of Man will send out his angels, and they will weed out of his kingdom everything that causes sin and all who do evil. They will throw them into the fiery furnace, where there will be weeping and gnashing of teeth. Then the righteous will shine like the sun in the kingdom of their*

Father. He who has ears let him hear (Matthew
13:37–43).

Jesus clearly states, *"The field is the world."* He then
explains that the wheat symbolizes the righteous and the tares
are the unrighteous, which must grow together until the
"harvest" at *"the end of the age."* *"The harvesters are the
angels"* who will separate the wheat from the tares at the
"harvest." We also notice that the angels of God are mentioned in association with the return of Christ. Compare the
verse above with the corresponding verse below from the
Olivet Discourse. Both refer to the time when Christ returns
to establish the Kingdom at the end of the age.

> *And he will send his angels with a loud trumpet
> call, and they will gather his elect from the four
> winds, from one end of the heavens to the other*
> (Matthew 24:31).

Jesus tells us that at the end of this age He will return
with His angels and gather the believers. We see the reward
of the righteous, *"Then the righteous will shine like the sun
in the Kingdom of their Father"* (Matthew 13:43). He also
tells us that the angels will separate out the unbelievers for
punishment: *"They will throw them into the fiery furnace,
where there will be weeping and gnashing of teeth"*
(Matthew 13:42). On the day the Son of Man comes there
will be deliverance for the righteous and punishment for the
disobedient. Notice the similarities between Matthew
13:43, above, and Daniel 12:3, below, as they describe the
deliverance of the believers:

> *Those who are wise will shine like the brightness of
> the heavens, and those who lead many to righteous-
> ness, like the stars for ever and ever* (Daniel 12:3).

Both verses depict the shining brightness of the believers when they receive their resurrection bodies and enter into the Kingdom of God at the end of the age.

The Parable of the Dragnet describes the same thing. The righteous will be gathered and the wicked will be separated out for punishment.

> *Once again, the kingdom of heaven is like a net that was let down into the lake and caught all kinds of fish. When it was full, the fishermen pulled it up on the shore. Then they sat down and collected the good fish in baskets, but threw the bad away. This is how it will be at the end of the age. The angels will come and separate the wicked from the righteous and throw them into the fiery furnace, where there will be weeping and gnashing of teeth* (Matthew 13:47–50).

From the Old Covenant to the New

Before we examine the Olivet Discourse, let's consider what was happening at this time in Jesus' ministry: Jesus had just made His triumphal entry into the holy city of Jerusalem, riding on the colt of a donkey in fulfillment of the prophecies in Zechariah 9:9 and Daniel 9:25. Jesus made one last attempt to get through to Israel's religious leaders; He continued to reveal who He was while instructing them regarding the coming Kingdom of God, using the parables of the landowner (Matthew 21:33–41), the wedding banquet (Matthew 22:1–14) and the resurrection of believers (Matthew 22:23–32). But the Herodians, the Sadducees and the Pharisees rejected the Messiah and plotted His death.

Jesus continued teaching them even though He knew their hearts. Then finally, He thoroughly admonished the elders, chief priests and teachers as He prepared to break with them. Jesus told of the coming destruction of Jerusalem and the temple. Just thirty-eight years later, in A.D. 70, this tremendous destruction and slaughter happened exactly as Jesus prophesied:

> *The days will come upon you when your enemies will build an embankment against you and encircle you and hem you in on every side. They will dash you to the ground, you and the children within your walls. They will not leave one stone on another,* **because** *you did not recognize the time of God's coming to you* (Luke 19:43,44).

We should note that Jesus said this destruction and slaughter would occur **because** the Jewish leaders did not recognize the time of His coming. Even though the Jewish leaders had all the Old Testament prophecies pointing to the coming Messiah, they did not recognize the time of His coming to them. Then, just before leaving the temple, Jesus prophesied again about Israel and His return: "*For I tell you, you will not see me again until you say, Blessed is he who comes in the name of the Lord*" (Matthew 23:38).

With this prophecy, Jesus, quoting from Psalm 118:26, laid down a condition of His return. Israel had to acknowledge Jesus as Lord before He would return and establish the Kingdom on earth.

The Olivet Discourse

Jesus' teaching of the last days, known as the Olivet Discourse, is recorded in each of the synoptic Gospels—Matthew 24, Mark 13 and Luke 21. It derives its name from the Mount of Olives—just across the Kidron Valley from the temple mount—where Jesus gave the discourse. In

His response to the disciples' question, Jesus Christ told of the events to precede His return and the end of the age.

> *Jesus left the temple and was walking away when his disciples came up to him to call his attention to its buildings. 'Do you see all these things?' he asked. 'I tell you the truth, not one stone here will be left on another; every one will be thrown down'* (Matthew 24:1,2).

While on the Mount of Olives, Peter, James, John and Andrew came to Him to ask one of the most important eschatological questions in Scripture: "*'Tell us,' they said, 'when will this happen, and what will be the sign of your coming* [parousia] *and the end of the age?'*" (Matthew 24:3).

In New Testament manuscripts, the Greek word *parousia* is that word most frequently used for the coming of Jesus Christ. It is first recorded here, in the disciples' question regarding Jesus' Second Coming. In His response to their question, *parousia* is recorded several times, signifying His arrival as He described the events leading up to His return.

In *Thayer's Greek-English Lexicon*, *parousia* is defined as "the presence of one coming, hence the coming, arrival, and Advent."[1] In today's North American English, we would most likely use the word "arrival" to convey the idea of *parousia*.

We need to understand the meaning of "*parousia*" as we read of "the coming" in our English Bible translations. The idea of coming often brings to mind the verb "to come," which describes an activity. *Parousia*, however, is a noun. It does not mean *the process* of coming; rather, it signifies *the event* of one's arrival. We will examine the meaning and significance of this in more detail later when we study the apostle Paul's writing.

Jesus' warning

Jesus' answer to the disciples' question provides a concise picture of what will happen between Jesus' departure and His return. Matthew's Gospel provides the most complete description of His response and is the Gospel we will use for understanding the return of Christ at the end of the age. We will now examine it verse by verse.

The very first thing Jesus addresses in His response is the issue of deception in the last days. He strongly warns the believers that they will need to be very careful: *"Watch out that no one deceives you. For many will come in my name, claiming, 'I am the Christ,' and will deceive many"* (Matthew 24:4,5).

Throughout the Olivet Discourse, Jesus warns the disciples about the deception that will come relating to the return of the Son of Man. The deception of believers and the need for spiritual alertness were two of Jesus' major concerns regarding the last days. Deception and false teaching are always concerns; however, Jesus' emphasis in connection to the last days should be cause for increased alertness. The apostles also echo Jesus' warnings about deception and false teaching in the church when they write about the last days. For example,

> *For the time will come when men will not put up with sound doctrine. Instead, to suit their own desires, they will gather around them a great number of teachers to say what their itching ears want to hear. They will turn their ears away from the truth and turn aside to myths* (2 Timothy 4:3,4).

After His initial warning, Jesus explains that, in the course of human history from His departure until His return, conflicts and wars are going to happen. However, he tells us not to be alarmed, for these things alone are not indications that the end of the age is near. "*You will hear of wars and rumors of wars, but see to it that you are not alarmed. Such things must happen, but the end is still to come*" (Matthew 24:6); "*When you hear of wars and revolutions, do not be frightened. These things must happen first, but the end will not come right away*" (Luke 21:9).

Beginning of birth pains

Next, Jesus describes several things that will take place and He says these will be the beginning of the events leading up to His return and the birth of the Kingdom of God.

> *Nation* [ethnos] *will rise against nation* [ethnos], *and kingdom against kingdom. There will be famines and earthquakes in various places. All these are the beginning of birth pains* (Matthew 24:7,8).

> *Then he said to them:* "*Nation* [ethnos] *will rise against nation* [ethnos], *and kingdom against kingdom. There will be great earthquakes, famines and pestilences in various places, and fearful events and great signs from heaven*" (Luke 21:10,11).

In these passages, the Greek word *ethnos* is translated as "*nation*"; however, an understanding of the Greek word *ethnos* may help us better understand what Jesus means when He tells *us* "ethnos *will rise against* ethnos." *Ethnos* means "a race (as of the same habit), i.e. a tribe; specifically a foreign (non-Jewish) one (usually by implication pagan):—Gentile, heathen, nation, people."[2] We get our English word *ethnic* from *ethnos*.

Therefore, Jesus is saying that ethnic group will rise against ethnic group and government will rise up against

government. He warns us that there will also be natural disasters, including famines, pestilences and earthquakes.[3] All
these things together will be the "*beginnings of birth
pains.*" This idea of birth pains is from the Old Testament,
where the Messiah's arrival is described as Israel *giving
birth* to the Kingdom of God. The concept of the deliverance of His people (Israel) through birth is described in
Isaiah 26:16–21, Isaiah 66:7–11 and Micah 5:2–4.

Many will turn away from the faith

After Jesus tells us about the beginning of the birth
pains, He warns of the persecution and death that will
occur, indicating that it is vitally important that we persevere and stand firm in the faith to the very end.

> *Then you will be handed over to be persecuted and
> put to death, and you will be hated by all nations
> because of me. At that time, many will turn away
> from the faith and will betray and hate each other,
> and many false prophets will appear and deceive
> many people. Because of the increase of wickedness,
> the love of most will grow cold, but he who stands
> firm to the end will be saved* (Matthew 24:9–13).

Tribulation and persecution have been part of the
believers' experience throughout this present age. Jesus
clearly taught that we are to expect persecution. For
example, in John 15:20, He said, "*Remember the words I
spoke to you: 'No servant is greater than his master.' If they
persecuted me, they will persecute you also.*" We are also
told to expect tribulation: "*I have told you these things, so
that in me you may have peace. In this world you will have
trouble* [tribulation]. *But take heart! I have overcome the
world*" (John 16:33).

We will also find the conditions described in Matthew 24:9–13 taking place during the time of persecution and deception Jesus called the *"great distress,"* in Matthew 24:21–25.

Conditions in the "great distress" or Great Tribulation:

1. Severe persecution and death.
2. Universal tribulation; you will be hated by all nations.
3. Great falling away from the faith.
4. False prophets and deception; many will be deceived.
5. There will be terrible times and increased wickedness.

Gospel proclaimed to all nations

In this next verse, Jesus indicates that the gospel of the Kingdom will be proclaimed worldwide and then the end will come: *"And this gospel of the kingdom will be preached in the whole world as a testimony to all nations, and then the end will come"* (Matthew 24:14).

Some have taught, using Matthew 24:14, that the coming of our Lord at the end of the age is dependent on the Church's preaching the gospel to all nations. While there is absolutely no doubt that we have clear instructions to make disciples of all nations, that is not the prophetic message of this verse. There is an important prophetic passage in Revelation that is clearly related to this prophecy. Let's compare the two and see.

> *Then I saw another angel flying in midair, and he had the eternal gospel to proclaim to those who live on the earth—to every nation, tribe, language and people. He said in a loud voice, 'Fear God and give him glory, because the hour of his judgment has come. Worship him who made the heavens, the earth, the sea and the springs of water'* (Revelation 14:6,7).

In the above description of last days, we find that an angel of the Lord will proclaim the eternal gospel to the whole world, in keeping with Jesus' prophecy in Matthew 24:14. Then following the proclamation to the whole world, we see the following—

> *I looked, and there before me was a white cloud, and seated on the cloud was one 'like a son of man' with a crown of gold on his head and a sharp sickle in his hand. Then another angel came out of the temple and called in a loud voice to him who was sitting on the cloud, 'Take your sickle and reap, because the time to reap has come, for the harvest of the earth is ripe.' So he who was seated on the cloud swung his sickle over the earth, and the earth was harvested* (Revelation 14:14–16).

Following the proclamation of the eternal gospel, the end will come, just as Jesus prophesies in Matthew 24:14. So far, Jesus is telling us what will happen all the way to the end of the age and the *harvest*.

The abomination that causes desolation

Starting in Matthew 24:15, Jesus is more detailed. After telling us generally what to watch for up to the end of the age, He returns to a specific event that will take place three and a half years before the end of the age. He begins by referring us to a key prophecy, which—when correctly understood—gives us a reference point for the last days' events. The prophecy in question pertains to the *abomination that causes desolation*.

> *So when you see standing in the holy place 'the abomination that causes desolation,' spoken of*

*through the prophet Daniel—**let the reader understand**—*(Matthew 24:15).

Jesus tells us that, if we are to comprehend what He is describing, we must understand the prophecies of Daniel. Daniel used the term *"abomination that causes desolation"* three times in his prophecies about the last days. In one of these prophecies, Daniel actually gives us the time frame of when this event will take place.

*He will confirm a covenant with many for one 'seven.'
In the middle of the 'seven' he will put an end to sacrifice and offering. And on a wing of the temple **he will
set up an abomination that causes desolation,** until the
end that is decreed is poured out on him* (Daniel 9:27).

Daniel tells us how the seven-year period will begin and how it will end. Daniel also describes an event, to take place in the middle of the seven years, which he calls an *"abomination that causes desolation."* We will study this important prophecy in detail in the next chapter.

Now that Jesus has told us about the *"abomination that causes desolation,"* He tells us what will happen immediately after that.

The Great Tribulation

Jesus tells us that at the time of the *"abomination that causes desolation,"* those who are in Judea—the area around Jerusalem—should flee to the mountains immediately:

*[T]hen let those who are in Judea flee to the moun-
tains. Let no one on the roof of his house go down
to take anything out of the house. Let no one in the
field go back to get his cloak. How dreadful it will
be in those days for pregnant women and nursing*

mothers! Pray that your flight will not take place in
winter or on the Sabbath (Matthew 24:16–20).

Following His warning for the people of God to flee
Judea immediately, Jesus describes a time of intense persecution and death that will come upon the whole world. This
is the time of the "*Great Tribulation,*" which Jesus says will
be so dreadful that there has never been anything like it in
the past and never will be anything like it in the future. Jesus
tells us that if the days of this persecution continued, no one
would survive. However, for the sake of the elect, the time
of "*Great Tribulation*" will be brought to a close before its
natural conclusion. The event that cuts short those days is
the return of the Son of Man.

In this passage, Jesus describes this period and identifies
the "*Great Tribulation*"—in the Greek, *megus thlipsis*:

> *For then there will be great* [megus] *distress*
> [thlipsis], *unequaled from the beginning of the*
> *world until now— and never to be equaled again. If*
> *those days had not been cut short, no one would*
> *survive, but for the sake of the elect those days will*
> *be shortened* (Matthew 24:21,22).

- *Megus* means big (literally or figuratively, in a very
  wide application): big (+ fear) exceedingly, **great** (-est),
  high, large, loud, mighty.[4]

- *Thlipsis* means pressure (literally or figuratively):
  afflicted, (-tion), anguish, burdened, persecution,
  tribulation, trouble.[5]

This three-and-a-half-year period is referred to as the
"*Great Tribulation,*" and we will use that term for the purposes of this study.

Notice that Jesus uses almost the same words to describe this period as Daniel did. Understanding that they are both referring to the same period of tribulation will be helpful as we continue our study. Jesus is ensuring that we make the connection with Daniel's prophecy. Compare the two and see: *"For **then there will be great distress, unequaled from the beginning of the world until now—** and never to be equaled again"* (Matthew 24:21).

> *At that time Michael, the great prince who protects your people, will arise. **There will be a time of distress such as has not happened from the beginning of nations until then.** But at that time your people— everyone whose name is found written in the book—will be delivered* (Daniel 12:1).

Another important similarity between these two passages is that Jesus and Daniel both tell us that the believers will be delivered after the Great Tribulation. Daniel says *"everyone whose name is found written in the book—*[of life] *will be delivered."* Jesus says *"Immediately after the distress of those days... they will see the Son of Man coming on the clouds... send his angels... they will gather his elect"* (Matthew 24:29–31).

More deception in the last days

As we return to the Olivet Discourse, once again Jesus is warning us of the great deception that will take place in the last days:

> *At that time, if anyone says to you, 'Look, here is the Christ!' or, 'There he is!' do not believe it. For false Christs and false prophets will appear and perform great signs and miracles to deceive even the*

*elect—if that were possible. See, I have told you
ahead of time. So if anyone tells you, 'There he is,
out in the desert,' do not go out; or, 'Here he is, in
the inner rooms,' do not believe it. For as lightning
that comes from the east is visible even in the west,
so will be the coming* [parousia] *of the Son of Man*
(Matthew 24:23–27).

Jesus says that the deception will be so great that even
the elect would be deceived *"if that were possible."*
However, the Bible seems clear on this point—true believers
will not be deceived. John makes a clear case that indicates
the elect will not be deceived.

*All inhabitants of the earth will worship the beast—
all whose names have not been written in the book
of life belonging to the Lamb that was slain from
the creation of the world* (Revelation 13:8).

Jesus continues His warning as He explains, in verse 24,
that false Christs and false prophets will appear to deceive
the elect. We know there have been imposters ever since
Christ's First Advent. However, the description Jesus gives
seems to tell of the rise of the final Antichrist and the False
Prophet (Revelation 16:13; 19:20). The deception in the last
days will be so great that Jesus finds it necessary to give us
this warning—*"See, I have told you ahead of time"*
(Matthew 24:25). He is clearly telling us that we are to wait
for His visible appearing in the clouds of the sky and His
physical return to earth.

   *"Wherever there is a carcass, there the vultures will
gather"* (Matthew 24:28); *"Where there is a dead body,
there the vultures will gather"* (Luke 17:37). The gathering
of the vultures is most likely a reference to the battle of

Armageddon, when the Lord slays the armies of the Antichrist and the birds of the air feed on their slain bodies. This is a picture portrayed several times in Scripture. For example, *"On the mountains of Israel you will fall, you and all your troops and the nations with you. I will give you as food to all kinds of carrion birds"* (Ezekiel 39:4); *"The rest of them were killed with the sword that came out of the mouth of the rider on the horse, and all the birds gorged themselves on their flesh"* (Revelation 19:21).

The sun, moon and stars are darkened

Once again, after bringing us right up to His arrival (*parousia*) in verse 27, Jesus stops and backs up to give us more details about the last days.

> *Immediately after the distress* [tribulation] *of those days* **'the sun will be darkened, and the moon will not give its light;** *the stars will fall from the sky, and the heavenly bodies will be shaken'* (Matthew 24:29).

Jesus explains that right after the Great Tribulation, we will see the sun, moon and stars being darkened. This is a sign that has been well established in the Old Testament in connection with the Day of the Lord. The sign of the sun, the moon and the stars being darkened is what the prophet Joel says will come **before** the Day of the Lord. See excerpts from Joel chapter 2:

> *Before them the earth shakes, the sky trembles, **the sun and moon are darkened, and the stars no longer shine.** The LORD thunders at the head of his army; his forces are beyond number, and mighty are those who obey his command. The day of the LORD is great; it is dreadful* (Joel 2:10,11).

"The sun will be turned to darkness and the moon to blood before the coming of the great and dreadful day of the LORD" (Joel 2:31). Jesus' use of this well-known Old Testament sign provides even more evidence that the Day of the Lord and return of Christ will follow the Great Tribulation, just as Jesus is telling us.

Son of Man coming in the clouds

At the time when the sun, moon and stars are darkened, Jesus says we will see the Son of Man coming on the clouds of the sky in great glory:

> *At that time the sign of the Son of Man will appear in the sky, and all the nations of the earth will mourn. They will see the Son of Man coming on the clouds of the sky, with power and great glory* (Matthew 24:30).

Christ's coming on the clouds of the sky is revealed by the Old Testament prophets and in the New Testament. Below are a few other examples that describe this coming of the Lord on the clouds.

> *He parted the heavens and came down; dark clouds were under his feet. He mounted the cherubim and flew; he soared on the wings of the wind. He made darkness his covering, his canopy around him— the dark rain clouds of the sky. Out of the brightness of his presence clouds advanced, with hailstones and bolts of lightning. The Lord thundered from heaven;* (Psalm 18:9–13).

> *"In my vision at night I looked, and there before me was one like a son of man, coming with the clouds of heaven* (Daniel 7:13); *"After that, we who are still alive and*

*are left will be caught up together with them in the clouds
to meet the Lord in the air"* (1 Thessalonians 4:17).

> *Look, he is coming with the clouds, and every eye
> will see him, even those who pierced him; and all the
> peoples of the earth will mourn because of him*
> (Revelation 1:7).

While Jesus gives us a good picture of His return in the
Olivet Discourse, when we add the other passages, the picture becomes extraordinary. Christ will come down from
heaven, appearing in brightness and glory, breaking out of
the darkness that will surround the earth.

He comes with all His angels

When Jesus tells us about His coming in the clouds of
the sky, He also mentions His angels. *"And he* [the Son of
Man] *will send his angels with a loud trumpet call, and they
will gather his elect"* (Matthew 24:31). His reference to the
presence of the angels at His coming is something Jesus
taught several times. See the following examples:

> *The harvest is the end of the age, and the harvesters
> are angels. As the weeds are pulled up and burned
> in the fire, so it will be at the end of the age. The
> Son of Man will send out his angels* (Matthew
> 13:39–41).

> *"When the Son of Man comes in his glory, and all the
> angels with him, he will sit on his throne in heavenly glory"*
> (Matthew 25:31).

> *If anyone is ashamed of me and my words, the Son
> of Man will be ashamed of him when he comes in
> his glory and in the glory of the Father and of the
> holy angels* (Luke 9:26).

The apostles also tell us that when Jesus appears, coming down from heaven, His angels will be with Him, "*thousands upon thousands.*" "*This will happen when the Lord Jesus is revealed from heaven in blazing fire with his powerful angels*" (2 Thessalonians 1:7); "*See, the Lord is coming with thousands upon thousands of his holy ones*" (Jude 1:14).

So, Jesus will appear in glory with "*thousands upon thousands*" of His holy angels, but another amazing event is about to happen.

The trumpet call

The scene is set. Jesus Christ will come down from heaven and appear out of the darkness on the clouds of the sky with many thousands of His angels. From there, Jesus says he will "*send his angels with a loud trumpet call, and they will gather his elect*" (Matthew 24:31).

Jesus points out that the trumpet call of God is the signal for the gathering of the saints. This trumpet call is an aspect of the coming of the Lord that is well established throughout Scripture. Below are several examples, which connect the Lord's appearing, and the trumpet call.

"*Then the LORD will appear over them; his arrow will flash like lightning. The Sovereign LORD will sound the trumpet*" (Zechariah 9:14); "*Blow the trumpet in Zion; sound the alarm on my holy hill. Let all who live in the land tremble, for the day of the LORD is coming*" (Joel 2:1).

For the Lord himself will come down from heaven, with a loud command, with the voice of the archangel and with the trumpet call of God, and the dead in Christ will rise first (1 Thessalonians 4:16).

Listen, I tell you a mystery: We will not all sleep, but we will all be changed— in a flash, in the twinkling of an eye, at the last trumpet. For the trumpet will sound, the dead will be raised imperishable, and we will be changed (1 Corinthians 15:51,52).

Many of the prophets have written of this trumpet call in connection with the return of the Lord. The trumpet call in relation to the coming of the Lord is first recorded in Exodus 19:16 and continues through Scripture all the way to Revelation 11:15–18. We will learn more about this trumpet call in subsequent chapters. For now we know it as the signal to gather Christ's elect.

His Elect

Jesus says that when He appears, He will send His angels to gather His elect. Who are *"his elect,"* those who will be gathered at the trumpet call? The word *elect* is translated from the Greek word *eklektos*.

Eklektos means select; by implication. favorite: chosen, elect.[6] *Eklektos* is used twenty-three times in the New Testament writings. *Eklektos* is used for believing Israel, the Church, the angels of God and even Christ Himself as the Chosen One of God. Let's look at a few examples. *"As you come to him, the living Stone—rejected by men but chosen* [eklektos] *by God and precious to him"* (1 Peter 2:4).

But you are a chosen [eklektos] *people, a royal priesthood, a holy nation, a people belonging to God, that you may declare the praises of him who called you out of darkness into his wonderful light. Once you were not a people, but now you are the people of God; once you had not received mercy, but now you have received mercy* (1 Peter 2:9,10).

The elect is also used in the Book of Revelation to refer to His called, chosen and faithful followers:

They will make war against the Lamb, but the Lamb will overcome them because he is Lord of lords and King of kings—and with him will be his called, chosen [eklektos] and faithful followers (Revelation 17:14).

From these examples we can see that *eklektos*, in Scripture, refers to all believers in Christ: Jewish and non-Jewish, Old Testament and New. Therefore, when Jesus tells us the angels will gather His elect when the trumpet sounds, He includes all true followers of Jesus Christ, everyone whose name is written in the *Book of Life*.

They are gathered from the earth and from heaven

Jesus tells us that when He appears, *"he will send his angels with a loud trumpet call, and they will gather his elect from the four winds, from one end of the heavens to the other"* (Matthew 24:31). What does Jesus mean when He says His elect will be gathered from the four winds and one end of the heavens to the other? Once again we need to search the Scripture to determine the answer.

Fortunately, several passages help us to correctly interpret to what Jesus refers as *"the four winds."* The best comparison is from the Gospel of Mark. Mark also wrote about this same part of the Olivet Discourse. *"And he will send his angels and gather his elect from the four winds, from the ends of the earth to the ends of the heavens"* (Mark 13:27).

Mark's version of the gathering of the elect reveals that *"the four winds"* refers to the earth. The term *"the four winds"* is also used to reference the earth in Revelation 7:1. *"The heavens"* in each verse refers to heaven. Therefore, the elect are gathered from the earth and from heaven.

King David, in Psalm 50, writes of the same event using similar wording to Matthew 24:30,31. Compare these two passages and see that they are describing the same thing:

*Our **God comes** and will not be silent; a fire devours before him, and around him a tempest rages. **He summons the heavens above, and the earth,** that he may judge his people: '**Gather to me my consecrated ones,** who made a covenant with me by sacrifice'* (Psalm 50:3–5).

*They will see the **Son of Man coming** on the clouds of the sky, with power and great glory. And **he will send his angels** with a loud trumpet call, and they will **gather his elect from the four winds, from one end of the heavens** to the other* (Matthew 24:30,31).

See how this is also confirmed by Paul's account of this gathering:

For the Lord himself will come down from heaven, with a loud command, with the voice of the archangel and with the trumpet call of God, and the dead in Christ will rise first. After that, we who are still alive and are left will be caught up together with them in the clouds to meet the Lord in the air. And so we will be with the Lord forever (1 Thessalonians 4:16,17).

Therefore, the Lord comes down from heaven on the clouds of the sky and we meet Him in the air. The heavens are above and the earth is below; the trumpet sounds, and He sends His angels to gather His elect. Who, then, are the ones being gathered from heaven?

From Paul's writing in 2 Corinthians 5:8, we see that when someone dies in Christ, they are at home with the Lord:

"We are confident, I say, and would prefer to be away from the body and at home with the Lord" (2 Corinthians 5:8).

We know Jesus is currently on the throne in heaven at the right hand of God the Father. We also know that the dead in Christ are with the Lord in heaven. Therefore, the dead in Christ will be in heaven until the time of the resurrection when Jesus summons them from heaven. Also, those who are still alive on the earth at that time will be caught up to meet the Lord in the air. Therefore, we can see at the time of the resurrection, Jesus will come down from heaven on the clouds of the sky, and from there He will send His angels to gather all believers to meet Him in the air.

Putting everything together, we can see the following sequence of events for the return of Christ:

1. Immediately after the *abomination that causes desolation*, there will be a Great Tribulation.
2. The Great Tribulation will be a time of persecution and death for the people of God, and great deception for the nations of the world.
3. After the Great Tribulation, the sun, moon and stars will be darkened.
4. Out of this darkness the Son of Man will appear coming on the clouds of the sky.
5. The trumpet will sound and angels will gather all believers—the dead from heaven and the living from earth.

Therefore, Jesus has told us that the resurrection of believers will take place after the Great Tribulation, or post-Tribulation.

When you see all these things

Now, let's return to the Olivet Discourse to see what else Jesus tells us about the last days.

*Now learn this lesson from the fig tree: As soon as its twigs get tender and its leaves come out, you know that summer is near. Even so, **when you see all these things, you know that it is near,** right at the door. I tell you the truth, this generation will certainly not pass away until all these things have happened* (Matthew 24:32–34).

This passage has confused some people, who have tried to add to Scripture by saying that the fig tree in this passage is the nation of Israel. However, that is not what Scripture says. This adding to the Word of God is dangerous and causes errors in interpretation. Errors in interpretation in turn lead to false teaching and deception. So, as cautioned in 1 Corinthians 4:6, *"Do not go beyond what is written."*

What can we conclude from this passage? Since Jesus often used farming examples in His teachings, the fig tree is most likely a fig tree. He is telling us that we can know about His coming, *"**when you see all these things, you know that it is near.**"* When we see what things? The things that He just finished telling us.

1. The *abomination that causes desolation.*
2. The *Great Tribulation.*
3. False Christ and the False Prophet.
4. The darkening of the sun, moon and stars.
5. The appearing of the Son of Man on the clouds of the sky.

Jesus seems to be saying that those who see these things (signs) will also see His coming. He is assuring us that, when this time of unequalled distress begins, the end of the age will come soon. After telling us how we can know the timing of His return, He goes on to tell us that we cannot know the day or hour of His return.

> *Heaven and earth will pass away, but my words will never pass away. 'No one knows about that day or hour, not even the angels in heaven, nor the Son, but only the Father'* (Matthew 24:35,36).

Jesus says we cannot know the day or hour of His return. However, Scripture clearly says we can know the general time or season of His return. In Hebrews, we are told we will see the day approaching:

> *Let us not give up meeting together, as some are in the habit of doing, but let us encourage one another— and all the more* **as you see the day approaching** (Hebrews 10:25).

Furthermore, Jesus commands us to *"keep watch"* and *"be alert!"* If we cannot know the signs of the times, why would Jesus say, *"When you see all these things, you know that it is near, right at the door"*? Why would Jesus, Paul and John each provide signs and events for us to watch for, if we cannot know the general time of Christ's return? See what they said: *"Therefore keep watch, because you do not know on what day your Lord will come"* (Matthew 24:42).

> *Don't let anyone deceive you in any way, for that day will not come until the rebellion occurs and the man of lawlessness is revealed, the man doomed to destruction* (2 Thessalonians 2:3).

"Dear children, this is the last hour; and as you have heard that the antichrist is coming…" (1 John 2:18).

These are just a few verses that tell us to be alert and watching for the signs we have been given. The apostle Paul tells us to watch for the rebellion and the Antichrist. John tells us the Antichrist is coming. These are signs we are to watch for!

As in the days of Noah

Jesus gives us another analogy of His return by referring us to Noah and his day. This is an example of how it will be at the return of the Lord: life will continue, with people concerned about the normal issues and cares up to the very end. Jesus says that, just as it was in the days of Noah, so it will be up to the Day of the Lord.

It is insightful to note that Noah is described, in 2 Peter 2:5, as *"a preacher of righteousness."* Apparently, Noah preached to the people of his day and warned them of the impending judgment. Yet, Jesus still says they knew nothing about what was going to happen. This would indicate that even though Noah preached to the people, they failed to believe and be saved. Therefore, they were all taken away in the judgment of the flood.

In this passage, Jesus makes a contrast between the believers and the unbelievers:

> *As it was in the days of Noah, so it will be at the coming of the Son of Man. For in the days before the flood, **people** were eating and drinking, marrying and giving in marriage, up to the day Noah entered the ark; and **they** knew nothing about what would happen until the flood came and took **them** all away. That is how it will be at the coming of the Son of Man* (Matthew 24:37–39).

Noah represents the believers. The others—*"people, they* and *them"*—represent the unbelievers. The believers—Noah and his family—were prepared. They knew what to do and when to do it. But the unbelievers, in spite of Noah's preaching, were caught off guard when the judgment was poured out on them. Jesus tells us that that is how it will be at the time of His return.

Compare what Jesus said with Paul's writing below.

> *For you know very well that the day of the Lord will come like a thief in the night. While **people** are saying, "Peace and safety," destruction will come on **them** suddenly, as labor pains on a pregnant woman, and **they** will not escape. But you, brothers, are not in darkness so that this day should surprise you like a thief* (1 Thessalonians 5:2–4).

The similarities in these two passages show that Paul and Jesus both refer to the return of Christ. Both passages assure us that the believers will not be caught unaware like the rest of the world. If we remain spiritually alert and watchful to the end, we will know the time of the Lord's arrival.

One taken, the other left

There is another message in this passage for which we need to look to the Greek. English translations alone do not provide a clear interpretation. Two very different Greek words are translated into a form of the English verb "to take." In verse 39, *airo* is translated as "*took.*" Then in verses 40 and 41, *paralambano* is translated as "*taken.*"

> *As it was in the days of Noah, so it will be at the coming of the Son of Man. For in the days before the flood, people were eating and drinking, marrying and giving in marriage, up to the day Noah entered the ark; and they knew nothing about what would happen until the flood came and **took** [airo] them all away. That is how it will be at the coming of the Son*

*of Man. Two men will be in the field; one will be **taken**
[paralambano] and the other left. Two women will be
grinding with a hand mill; one will be **taken** [par-
alambano] and the other left* (Matthew 24:37–41).

The difference between these Greek words is important.

- *Airo* means "to take away, put away, loose, and
  remove."[7]

- *Paralambano* means "to receive near, i.e., associate
  with oneself (in any familiar or intimate act or relation); receive, take unto, take with."[8]

These two Greek words actually have opposite mean-
ings! Though it is rare that good English translations are
misleading, we should be alert to the possibility. Looking to
the Greek is often useful when there is a disagreement over
a doctrinal issue, such as the return of Jesus Christ.

Therefore, we are told that when Jesus returns, the
believers will be taken unto the Lord or received unto the
Lord, because *paralambano* means to receive. A corresponding verse in the Gospel of John lends further support
to this understanding: "*And if I go and prepare a place for
you, I will come back and **take** [paralambano] **you to be
with me** that you also may be where I am*" (John 14:3).

This verse refers to the same event and employs the
same Greek word, *paralambano*. In each case, these passages describe the same event that Paul describes below
when he tells us we will be gathered together to meet the
Lord and we will be with Him forever.

*For the Lord himself will come down from heaven,
with a loud command, with the voice of the archangel
and with the trumpet call of God, and the dead in
Christ will rise first. After that, we who are still alive*

*and are left will be caught up together with them in the clouds to meet the Lord in the air. And so **we will be with the Lord forever** (1 Thessalonians 4:16,17).*

Therefore, when the Lord returns, one man in the field will be received unto the Lord and the other will be put away from Him. One woman will be gathered unto the Lord in the air and the other will be left to the judgment and wrath of God.

Once again, Scripture presents a clear and consistent picture of the return of Christ. Jesus will return at the end of the age, separate the believers from the unbelievers, gather the believers to Himself and leave the unbelievers to suffer His wrath. Once again we see that the resurrection of believers (the living and the dead) will occur at the end of the age, immediately after the Great Tribulation.

Therefore keep watch

In the next verses, Jesus commands us to be spiritually alert and warns of the consequences of not being ready. Let's look at this section a few verses at a time.

Therefore keep watch, because you do not know on what day your Lord will come. But understand this: If the owner of the house had known at what time of night the thief was coming, he would have kept watch and would not have let his house be broken into. So you also must be ready, because the Son of Man will come at an hour when you do not expect him (Matthew 24:42–44).

Jesus is telling us to be aware of what is going on and to be knowledgeable regarding the signs of His return. We must always be ready, because we will not know the day or hour of His arrival. However, this is more than a command to be watchful—it is also a warning to be spiritually alert. Sadly, many people today are not watching and are not ready. Some have even been told there is nothing to watch for, because Jesus could come at any moment.

> *Who then is the faithful and wise servant, whom the master has put in charge of the servants in his household to give them their food at the proper time? It will be good for that servant whose master finds him doing so when he returns. I tell you the truth, he will put him in charge of all his possessions* (Matthew 24:45–47).

We know that Jesus has put overseers, elders, pastors and teachers in charge of His household to give His people their food at the proper time: "*It is written: 'Man does not live on bread alone, but on every word that comes from the mouth of God'*" (Matthew 4:4). These leaders are responsible to provide the Word of God, regarding the return of Christ, at the proper time. If they do so, they will be greatly rewarded. However, if they do not heed this warning and command from the Lord, there will be consequences.

> *But suppose that servant is wicked and says to himself, 'My master is staying away a long time,' and he then begins to beat his fellow servants and to eat and drink with drunkards. The master of that servant will come on a day when he does not expect him and at an hour he is not aware of. He will cut him to pieces and assign him a place with the hypocrites, where there will be weeping and gnashing of teeth* (Matthew 24:48–51).

As we can see, those who busy themselves with the things and the cares of this world instead of providing the

Word of God will be punished. He will come when they do not expect Him and He will treat them as unbelievers.

Parable of the Ten Virgins

The last part of the Olivet Discourse contains the Parable of the Ten Virgins and the Parable of the Talents. In both parables, Jesus reminds us to stay spiritually alert and obedient to God and also tells us we should be prepared to wait a long time.

At that time the kingdom of heaven will be like ten virgins who took their lamps and went out to meet the bridegroom. Five of them were foolish and five were wise. The foolish ones took their lamps but did not take any oil with them. The wise, however, took oil in jars along with their lamps. The bridegroom was a long time in coming, and they all became drowsy and fell asleep. At midnight the cry rang out: 'Here's the bridegroom! Come out to meet him!' Then all the virgins woke up and trimmed their lamps. The foolish ones said to the wise, 'Give us some of your oil; our lamps are going out.' 'No,' they replied, 'there may not be enough for both us and you. Instead, go to those who sell oil and buy some for yourselves.' But while they were on their way to buy the oil, the bridegroom arrived. The virgins who were ready went in with him to the wedding banquet. And the door was shut. Later the others also came. 'Sir! Sir!' they said. 'Open the door for us!' But he replied, 'I tell you the truth, I don't know you.' Therefore keep watch, because you do not know the day or the hour (Matthew 25:1–13).

In this parable, Jesus describes the professing church as waiting for the Lord's return. We know the ten virgins represent the professing church, because the world is not waiting for the return of Jesus Christ. The foolish virgins represent the part of the professing church that does not have a personal relationship with Christ, because when He returns he says, *"I don't know you."* The wise virgins, on the other hand, are the true Church, because God knows and has a personal relationship with them. This parable seems to imply that about half the professing church are unsaved and do not have a saving relationship with Jesus Christ.

Again Jesus states that he will be gone a long time, as He did in Matthew 25:5. It has been almost 2,000 years since our Lord returned to heaven to sit at the right hand of God the Father. The message that He will be gone a long time seems to have a dual meaning. First, that we must be prepared to wait and persevere until Christ's return. The other meaning is that He will be gone a long time—almost 2,000 years so far.

"After a long time the master of those servants returned and settled accounts with them" (Matthew 25:19). While the Lord is going to be gone for a long time, He will assuredly return, and when He does, He will establish the Kingdom of God on earth. Before he establishes the Kingdom on earth, His angels will separate the wicked from the righteous. *"And throw that worthless servant outside, into the darkness, where there will be weeping and gnashing of teeth"* (Matthew 25:30).

Faith that works

The remaining parables in Matthew 25 instruct us regarding the importance of having a "faith that works." Merely knowing of Jesus is not sufficient. In each case, those who did not put their faith into action were left to suffer eternal punishment. These teachings vividly demonstrate, in accord with the instructions in the epistle of James, that faith without works is dead.

We have now completed our study of the complete picture of the return of Christ, as given by Jesus Christ Himself. We will now go on from Jesus' teachings to study what the apostles and prophets wrote, starting with the prophet Daniel.

CHAPTER THREE

Spoken of Through the Prophet Daniel

*So when you see standing in
the holy place 'the abomination that
causes desolation,' spoken of through
the prophet Daniel—let the reader
understand* (Matthew 24:15).

As we recall in the Olivet Discourse, Matthew 24:15, Jesus directs our attention to the prophet Daniel. By referring to Daniel, Jesus draws our attention to prophecies that detail the timing and sequence of the last days' events. Daniel's prophecies were written during the sixth century B.C., after the Babylonians had conquered Israel and taken the Israelites into captivity. Daniel received several visions and prophecies during this time, beginning when he was a youth under the rule of King Nebuchadnezzar of Babylon.

Daniel's first vision and prophecy was regarding a dream received by King Nebuchadnezzar. Daniel received the vision of this dream and its interpretation from God. The vision revealed that four world kingdoms would come to power before God established His Kingdom on earth.

The first of the four kingdoms was Babylon, which fell to the second kingdom of Medo-Persia. After the kingdom of Medo-Persia, the third kingdom of Greece came to power under Alexander the Great. Daniel's prophecies also revealed the identity of these first three kingdoms.

> *The two-horned ram that you saw represents the kings of **Media and Persia**. The shaggy goat is the king of **Greece**, and the large horn between his eyes is the first king* (Daniel 8:20,21).

After the first three world kingdoms had risen and fallen, another kingdom appeared—Rome. While Rome seemed to fulfill some aspects of Daniel's prophecy regarding the fourth kingdom, it did not fulfill all that was written. Since Rome did not fulfill all that was written regarding the fourth beast kingdom, we can be sure that there will be another kingdom that will fulfill these prophecies. Therefore, Daniel's prophecy regarding the fourth kingdom is for the future.

Following the fall of Babylon and during the first year of the reign of Darius the Mede, Daniel received from God one of the most amazing prophecies of the Bible. This prophecy we will refer to as Daniel's *"Seventy Sevens"* prophecy. The specific information provided in this prophecy enables us to determine the exact time of the First Coming of Christ as King. This same prophecy also provides several details describing key events of the last seven years of Daniel's prophecy, which we call Daniel's seventieth week. First, we will examine the prophecy regarding the coming of Christ as King, and then we will study the last seven-year period.

At the time Darius ruled from Babylon, Daniel came to understand, from the prophecy of Jeremiah 25:11, that the desolation of Jerusalem would last seventy years (Daniel

9:1,2). When Daniel realized the desolation of Jerusalem was coming to a close, he began to seek the Lord in prayer and to petition for the restoration of Jerusalem and the temple. While Daniel was praying, he received the *"Seventy Sevens"* prophecy, which he was told to consider and understand.

The *"Seventy Sevens"* prophecy consists of four verses which have astounded scholars and students for centuries. So accurate are the details of this prophecy that skeptics have insisted the Book of Daniel must have been written after Christ's First Coming. However, since the discoveries between 1948 and 1952 of the Dead Sea Scrolls, the skeptics have been relatively quiet on this topic. The Dead Sea Scrolls discoveries included the Book of Daniel, and it has been determined that these predated Christ by at least 200 years. Therefore, these discoveries have provided archeological evidence confirming that the prophecies of Daniel predated Christ's First Coming.

Now, let's turn to Daniel's *"Seventy Sevens"* prophecy. As Daniel was given this prophecy, he was commanded to know and understand this vision and prophecy two times. *"Therefore, consider the message and understand the vision"* (Daniel 9:23); *"Know and understand this"* (Daniel 9:25).

The command to understand this prophecy was later repeated by Christ when He commanded, *"let the reader understand"* (Matthew 24:15). Therefore, in case we might miss the importance of this prophecy, God has commanded us to know and understand it no less than three times in His Word. Needless to say, this prophecy is very important.

Now, as we consider this vision, we find that the first verse establishes the time frame of this prophecy:

Seventy 'sevens' [shabuwa] are decreed for your people and your holy city to finish transgression, to

*put an end to sin, to atone for wickedness, to bring
in everlasting righteousness, to seal up vision and
prophecy and to anoint the most holy* (Daniel 9:24).

In Hebrew, *shabuwa* is translated "*sevens.*" "*Shabuwa*
means sevened, seven or a week."[1] The fulfillment of the
first part of this prophecy in history has verified that the
meaning of *shabuwa*, here, means seven years. As we will
shortly see, the first sixty-nine of the "*seventy sevens*" have
been fulfilled exactly as prophesied. So, we know with certainty that *shabuwa*, in Daniel's "*Seventy Sevens*" prophecy,
means seven years *and* "*seventy sevens*" equals 490 years.
Therefore, 490 years are decreed for "your people and your
holy city," Jerusalem, to:

1. Finish transgression.
2. End sin.
3. Atone for wickedness.
4. Bring in everlasting righteousness.
5. Seal up vision and prophecy.
6. Anoint the most holy.

These six items list what the prophecy says will be
accomplished for the people of God and the holy city
(Jerusalem) at the conclusion of the 490 years. While we
could debate whether or not Christ accomplished some of
these things on the cross, it is evident that not all these things
have been fulfilled at the present time. For example,
regarding the sealing up of prophecy, Scripture reveals that
prophecy will continue to the very end of the age, because it
is written that the two witnesses will prophesy for 1,260
days—see Revelation 11:3. Therefore, *since prophecy has not
yet been sealed up, the final fulfillment of Daniel's "Seventy
Sevens"* is still in the future. And even though Christ paid the

atonement price for sin, we still see that sin is present and everlasting righteousness has not yet been achieved.

Daniel 9:24 indicates that after 490 years, God will restore everything to His people and His holy city Jerusalem.

■ FROM THE DECREE—MARCH 14, 445 B.C.

As we have seen in Daniel 9:25, God says that we are to "know and understand this," because with this prophecy, the people of God would be able determine the exact time of the coming of the Messiah. We have already seen, from His statements to the Jewish leaders in Luke 19:44, that Jesus expected them to have known the time of His coming. We already know that the entire prophecy is 490 years in duration. Therefore, we now need to know when the 490 years begins. Daniel provides the answer in this verse:

> *Know and understand this: From the issuing of the decree to restore and rebuild Jerusalem until the Anointed One* [Messiah], *the ruler* [King], *comes, there will be seven 'sevens,' and sixty-two 'sevens.' It will be rebuilt with streets and a trench, but in times of trouble* (Daniel 9:25).

Daniel tells us that there will be a decree to restore and rebuild Jerusalem. Also implied in the rebuilding of Jerusalem is the rebuilding of the temple. We know this because Daniel was seeking God in prayer for the restoration of Jerusalem and the temple (Daniel 9:17–18) and because, when the decree was issued, it included Jerusalem and the temple.

There has, however, been debate over the years about which decree started the timing for this prophecy. There were a total of four decrees issued to rebuild the temple. The first three decrees called for the rebuilding of only the temple, and they are recorded in the Book of Ezra: Ezra 1:1–4 (Cyrus mentions only the temple); Ezra 6:1–12 (mentions the decree to rebuild the temple issued by Darius Hystaspis); and Ezra 7:11–26 (records the third decree, issued by Artaxerxes Lonimanus during the seventh year of his reign). These decrees called for the rebuilding of the temple; the rebuilding of Jerusalem was not included in any of the first three.

However, a fourth decree *did* call for the rebuilding of Jerusalem. This decree, which is recorded in Nehemiah 2:5–18, allows us to identify the exact date when this prophecy of the "seventy sevens" begins. This decree was made on March 14, 445 B.C.[2]

Remember, from verse twenty-six that, from the time of the decree to restore and rebuild Jerusalem, there will be *"seven sevens"* and "sixty-two sevens," or sixty-nine *"sevens"* (483 years) until "the anointed one, the ruler" comes.

So that we understand clearly whom this prophecy is about, let's look at the Hebrew words for *"the anointed one, the ruler."* "The Hebrew word *mashiyach*[3] means, *"anointed one"* and *nagiyd*[4] means "ruler, prince or leader." The Hebrew word *mashiyach* is where we get the word *Messiah*. *Nagiyd* was the title used to refer to Saul, the first King of Israel, in Samuel 9:16. Therefore, it would also be correct to translate *mashiyach nagiyd* as "Messiah the King." If we were to put "Messiah the King" into New Testament terms, we would say *"Christ the King."* Therefore, this verse tells us that from the decree until Christ the King comes, there will be 483 years.

To understand the time period of this prophecy, we will refer to the work of Sir Robert Anderson, who first published his classic study on the interpretation of Daniel's prophecy, titled the *The Coming Prince*, in 1895.[5] In his research, Anderson demonstrated that the time from the decree in March 14, 445 B.C. to April 6, A.D. 32 was exactly 483 years to the day. The calculation was made using the Jewish calendar at the time of the prophecy, which contained 360 days. The scholarship of Anderson's work was so sound that his book continues to be an authoritative work and is still being reprinted today.

■ To the Messiah the King—April 6, A.D. 32

At the time of Christ's First Advent, some of the Jewish people understood that Daniel's prophecy would find its fulfillment with the coming of the Messiah the King. Scripture was clear that the Messiah would reign over the people of the earth from David's throne at the restoration of all things. For example:

> *Of the increase of his government and peace there will be no end. He will reign on David's throne and over his kingdom, establishing and upholding it with justice and righteousness from that time on and forever* (Isaiah 9:7).

They also knew that the reign of Christ would be a time of righteousness and all nations of the earth would live in peace. That is what the Jewish people were waiting for as they looked forward to the coming of the Messiah the King. Because of the details of Daniel's prophecy, they also had a very good idea when the Messiah was to be expected. That is very likely why we find in the Gospels that the whole nation of Israel was looking for the Messiah at the very time of Christ's First Advent. They knew, just as we know today, that the prophecies of Scripture cannot be broken and all Scripture must be fulfilled as it is written. The Messiah was coming to fulfill prophecy at the appointed time. So, how do we know that April 6, A.D. 32 was the correct time for the Messiah's coming? Good question! How does the Bible answer this question? April 6, A.D. 32 is the date Jesus rode the colt of a donkey into Jerusalem, on what we call Palm Sunday.

From before Jesus' First Advent, He was destined to be King, but the timing of His coming as King could only be at the appointed time as foretold in the Scripture. As we read through the Gospels, we find times when the people wanted to take Jesus and make Him King, but He would not allow it. Then one day He began to make specific arrangements to fulfill the timing of the prophets, just as written. Both King David and Zechariah prophesied of the coming Messiah, allowing us to determine the circumstances that would take place at the time of the King's arrival.

Look at the picture David portrays in this psalm. He writes an account of the Lord's entry into the holy city of Jerusalem, complete with festival procession, boughs being waved and shouts of "*save us.*" David even seems to prophesy the sacrifice that would follow when he writes, "*to the horns of the altar.*" This indicates that Jesus was going to make a sacrifice. At "*the horns of the altar,*" the atonement for sin was made.

> *This is the day the LORD has made; let us rejoice and be glad in it. O LORD, save us; O LORD, grant us success. Blessed is he who comes in the name of the LORD. From the house of the LORD we bless you. The LORD is God, and he has made his light shine upon us. With boughs in hand, join in the festal procession up to the horns of the altar* (Psalm 118:24–27).

This is an amazingly descriptive prophecy showing Jesus Christ coming to the house of the Lord in Jerusalem and His subsequent sacrifice. This and several other prophecies substantiate that this was the appointed time for the coming of the Messiah the King.

Zechariah also prophesied about the coming King, saying He would enter Jerusalem riding on the colt of a donkey. When we compare these prophecies with the record of their fulfillment, there can be no doubt that this is the coming of Messiah, as foretold in Daniel 9:25.

> *Rejoice greatly, O Daughter of Zion! Shout, Daughter of Jerusalem! See, your king comes to you, righteous and having salvation, gentle and riding on a donkey, on a colt, the foal of a donkey* (Zechariah 9:9).

The crowds in Jerusalem shouted, "Hosanna to the Son of David!" *Hosanna* means "save" and the "Son of David" is a reference to the Messiah. In Psalm 118:25, there is a festival procession with people shouting, "save us, O Lord." Compare these passages and see the fulfillment marking the exact date of Daniel 9:25. Jesus Christ offered Himself as King when He entered Jerusalem on April 6, A.D. 32. This is how the prophesied event is recorded in the Gospel of Matthew:

> *This took place to fulfill what was spoken through the prophet: "Say to the Daughter of Zion, 'See, your king comes to you, gentle and riding on a donkey, on a colt, the foal of a donkey'"...They brought the donkey and the colt, placed their cloaks on them, and Jesus sat on them. A very large crowd spread their cloaks on the road, while others cut branches from the trees and spread them on the road. The crowds that went ahead of him and those that followed shouted, "Hosanna to the Son of David!" "Blessed is he who comes in the name of the Lord!" "Hosanna in the highest!" When Jesus*

entered Jerusalem, the whole city was stirred and asked, "Who is this?" (Matthew 21:4–10).

If only they had known the time of His coming and had recognized the Messiah the King! Jesus even seems to have confirmed that this was indeed the exact day that had been prophesied when He said, as He was approaching Jerusalem, *"If you, even you, had only known **on this day** what would bring you peace—but now it is hidden from your eyes"* (Luke 19:42).

Jesus makes a covenant by sacrifice

After Jesus rode into Jerusalem and offered himself as the Messiah the King, Daniel says that the Messiah would be *"cut off"*—*"After the sixty-two 'sevens,' the Anointed One will be cut off* [karath] *and will have nothing"* (Daniel 9:26a).

When Daniel writes that after the *"sixty-two sevens"* which follow the *"seven sevens"* (in Daniel 9:25), he is saying that after the *"sixty-nine sevens"* the Messiah will be cut off. Therefore, after Jesus' coming on April 6, A.D. 32, Daniel tells us that the Messiah the King will be cut off. This corresponds exactly to the Gospel account which indicates that Jesus went to the cross and was crucified just days after his triumphal entry into Jerusalem.

To understand what is being prophesied, it will be helpful to understand what is meant by the term *"cut off."* Almost every English Bible translation of Daniel 9:26 renders the Hebrew word *karath* as "cut off." Since the term "cut off" seems a bit obscure, we might ask what is the meaning of the word *karath*? According to *Strong's Concordance,* *"karath* means to make a covenant (i.e. make an alliance or bargain, orig. by cutting flesh and passing between the pieces)."[6] In other words, *karath* means to make a covenant by sacrifice.

Now, we know from Scripture that after the coming of the Messiah, He laid down His life as an offering for the forgiveness of sin: *"Just as Christ loved us and gave himself up for us as a fragrant offering and sacrifice to God"* (Ephesians 5:2).

So, what is the connection between the Hebrew word *karath* and the sacrifice Christ made for sin? The meaning of *karath* is a perfect description of what Jesus Christ did when He went to the cross. Since *karath* means to make a covenant by sacrifice, we can understand Daniel 9:26 to say, *[a]fter 483 years, Messiah the King will make a covenant by sacrifice and will have nothing*. Which is exactly what we see happened after Jesus Christ entered Jerusalem on April 6, A.D. 32. He then made a covenant, in His own blood on the cross, for the forgiveness of sin. This covenant for the forgiveness of sin is still available today for all who would receive it by faith.

Destruction of Jerusalem and the temple

Next, Daniel tells us that after the Messiah makes a covenant by sacrifice, the people of the ruler who will come will destroy Jerusalem and the temple.

> *The people of the ruler who will come will destroy the city and the sanctuary. The end will come like a flood: War will continue until the end, and desolations have been decreed* (Daniel 9:26b).

Jesus also predicted this same destruction of Jerusalem and the temple when He told the chief priests and the teachers of the law that this destruction would be the result of their failing to know and understand this prophecy. Remember, God had told them, in Daniel 9:25, to *"know and understand."* And they did not!

*The days will come upon you when your enemies will build an embankment against you and encircle you and hem you in on every side. They will dash you to the ground, you and the children within your walls. They will not leave one stone on another, **because you did not recognize the time of God's coming to you*** (Luke 19:43,44).

In A.D. 70, just as Jesus and Daniel predicted, the Roman army under general Titus came to besiege Jerusalem.[7] The Jewish historian Flavius Josephus documented this event, estimating that 1,100,000 Jews were killed in the destruction of Jerusalem and the temple.[8] He recorded that the Roman army set fire to the temple, causing the gold in the temple to melt down into the cracks of the stonework. The Roman army then took down every stone, one from another, to get the gold—just as Jesus had predicted (Luke 19:44).

After Daniel predicts the destruction of Jerusalem and the temple in verse twenty-six, he says, *"The end will come like a flood: War will continue until the end, and desolations have been decreed."* This description sounds much like the description Jesus gave us in the Olivet Discourse for the time between His first and second Advents. Jesus said, *"You will hear of war and rumors of wars, ...but the end is still to come"* (Matthew 24:6).

■ INTERRUPTION IN DANIEL'S 70 WEEKS

So, at this point, 483 years of the 490-year prophecy have already been fulfilled. Now, if the last seven years of the 490-year prophecy had run continuously, they would have been completed from A.D. 32 to 39. However, thirty-eight more years elapsed before the destruction of Jerusalem in A.D. 70 and the final seven years of the prophecy still remained unfulfilled.

In the timeline below, there is a depiction of Daniel's Seventy Sevens prophecy with the interruption between the first sixty-nine *"sevens"* and the last *"seven."*

Daniel's Seventy Sevens = 490 years

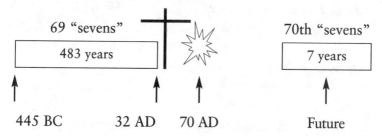

Note: *The reason 445 B.C. plus 32 A.D. doesn't equal 483 years is due to changes in the calendars.*

The interruption in this prophecy is not unique to Scripture. As a matter of fact, the interruption between the two Advents of Christ is actually found several times in Scripture. One example comes from John the Baptist when he describes two aspects of the ministry of Jesus. *"He will baptize you with the Holy Spirit* [**interruption**] *and with fire"* (Matthew 3:11). This prophecy from John the Baptist reveals that Jesus will first baptize us with the Holy Spirit, which He fulfilled on the day of Pentecost almost 2,000 years ago. The second part of this prophecy states that He will baptize us with fire, which He will do on the Day of the Lord when Jesus will judge His people by fire. See how Paul describes this below:

> *Every man's work shall be made manifest: for the day shall declare it, because it shall be revealed by fire; and the fire shall try every man's work of what sort it is. If any man's work abide which he hath built thereupon,*

he shall receive a reward. If any man's work shall be burned, he shall suffer loss: but he himself shall be saved; yet so as by fire (1 Corinthians 3:13–15).

Another example is found in the Gospel of Luke. Jesus revealed that He was fulfilling Scripture in the people's hearing when He read from the prophecies of Isaiah. He did not, however, finish reading the complete prophecy as recorded in Isaiah 61. He stopped in mid-sentence at the point where it says "*the Lord's favor.*" The reason He did not continue reading the remainder of Isaiah's prophecy is because the remainder of the prophecy, just as we have seen in John the Baptist's prophecy above, would not be fulfilled until His return on the Day of the Lord. Compare the passage in Luke's record with Isaiah's prophecy and see the interruption between the first and second Advents of Christ.

'*The Spirit of the Lord is on me, because he has anointed me to preach good news to the poor. He has sent me to proclaim freedom for the prisoners and recovery of sight for the blind, to release the oppressed, to proclaim the year of the* LORD'*s favor.* [**interruption**] *Then he rolled up the scroll gave it back to the attendant and sat down. The eyes of everyone in the synagogue were fastened on him, and he began by saying to them, 'Today this scripture is fulfilled in your hearing*' (Luke 4:18–21).

To proclaim the year of the LORD'*s favor* [**interruption**] *and the day of vengeance of our God, to comfort all who mourn, and provide for those who grieve in Zion* (Isaiah 61:2,3).

Jesus fulfilled the first part of Isaiah's prophecy—"*the*

year of the LORD's *favor"*—at His First Coming. The second part, *"the day of vengeance,"* Jesus will fulfill at His Second Coming on the Day of the Lord.

As we can see, these prophecies have two parts with an interruption separating the two Advents of Christ. The first part of each was fulfilled about 2,000 years ago, in relationship to Christ's First Coming; the second part will be fulfilled at the Christ's Second Coming on the Day of the Lord.

We are currently living during the time of the interruption between the two Advents of Christ. We also know that several prophesied events have already occurred during this interruption period. The first was when Jesus made the New Covenant in His blood on the cross. The next was the destruction of Jerusalem and the temple in A.D. 70, and recently, Israel's restoration to their land as a nation on May 14, 1948 is most likely a fulfillment of biblical prophecy.

> *The days are coming, declares the* LORD, *when I will bring my people Israel and Judah back from captivity and restore them to the land I gave their forefathers to possess, says the* LORD (Jeremiah 30:3).

> *Therefore say: 'This is what the Sovereign* LORD *says: I will gather you from the nations and bring you back from the countries where you have been scattered, and I will give you back the land of Israel again'* (Ezekiel 11:17).

This brings us to Daniel's seventieth week, a key to understanding the last days and the return of Christ.

■ DANIEL'S SEVENTIETH WEEK

Now that we have reviewed the completed portion of Daniel's Seventy Sevens prophecy, let's read of the final seven-year period. Below is the verse which describes the details of Daniel's seventieth week and a timeline depicting the key events of that period.

> *He will confirm a covenant with many for one 'seven.' In the middle of the 'seven' he will put an end to sacrifice and offering. And on a wing of the temple he will set up an abomination that causes desolation, until the end that is decreed is poured out on him* (Daniel 9:27).

Last Days Timeline

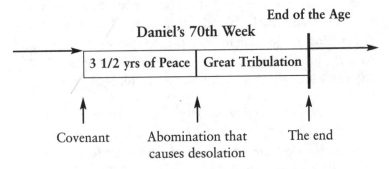

He will confirm a covenant

Because of the importance of this prophecy, we will break it down into its component parts to see each element of what will take place as the world moves through these last days toward the return of Christ.

"*He will confirm a covenant with many for one 'seven'*" (Daniel 9:27a). The "*He*" in this verse is a pronoun referring to the ruler in the previous verse (Daniel 9:26). As we have already seen, the ruler was the Roman general Titus. Titus and the Roman army fulfilled the part of the prophecy about the destruction of Jerusalem; however, Titus did not fulfill the rest of this prophecy. Therefore, Titus is not the fulfillment of this prophecy—he is only a "type" of the world leader who will come in the last days. This means the *"He"* in Daniel 9:27 refers to the future world leader who will come. This will be the world leader referred to in Scripture as *"the beast," "the antichrist"* and the *"man of lawlessness"* (2 Thessalonians 2:3).

Before we continue our examination of Daniel's seventieth week, we will first examine Daniel's prophecies relating to the "fourth beast kingdom." For it is out of this fourth beast kingdom that the Antichrist will rise to power in the last days.

The fourth beast kingdom

Daniel wrote several times about the four beast kingdoms that would arise on the earth. In the first year of Belshazzar's reign over Babylon, Daniel had a dream which provided an apocalyptic picture of the four beast kingdoms that would to rise to power on the earth. During the time of that vision, he was also given an explanation of its meaning. In Daniel 7:23–24, the brief but insightful explanation of that vision is recorded for us.

> *He gave me this explanation: 'The fourth beast is a fourth kingdom that will appear on earth. It will be different from all the other kingdoms and will devour the whole earth, trampling it down and crushing it.' The ten horns are ten kings who will come from this kingdom. After them another king will arise, different from the earlier ones; he will subdue three kings* (Daniel 7:23, 24).

Here the Lord has given us a description of what He calls the fourth beast kingdom. We are told it will be different from the earlier kingdoms of Babylon, Medo-Persia and

Greece. One of the differences is that this last beast kingdom will have power and dominion over the whole earth. Another difference is revealed in a previous prophecy of Daniel. This final beast kingdom will be a kingdom of diverse nations and this diversity will be both a source of its strength and cause of its weakness: "...*will be a mixture and will not remain united*" (Daniel 2:42,43).

The fourth beast kingdom will originally be composed of ten leaders. Then another leader will arise and take the place of one of the original ten. This new leader will be different from the original ten, because of his superior ambition and ability. He will then conquer three of the original leaders, leaving the fourth beast kingdom with seven heads. The fourth beast kingdom will then have "*seven heads and ten horns.*" This new leader who rises from within the fourth beast kingdom will be the beast also known as the Antichrist. Therefore, when it is written that the fourth beast kingdom has "*seven heads and ten horns,*" we will know that the Antichrist will be leading that kingdom. See Revelation 17:4.

Rise of the Antichrist

Daniel received many prophecies during his time in Babylon relating to the Antichrist, whom he called the beast (Daniel 7:11). Daniel's prophecies provide insight into some of the political, military and religious conditions of the times as well as revealing various aspects of the character and nature of the Antichrist. Below are examples of Daniel's prophecies that give us insight into the character of this coming world leader:

> *He will speak against the Most High and oppress his saints and try to change the set times and the*

laws. The saints will be handed over to him for a time, times and half a time [three and a half years] (Daniel 7:25).

He will become very strong, but not by his own power. He will cause astounding devastation and will succeed in whatever he does. He will destroy the mighty men and the holy people. He will cause deceit to prosper, and he will consider himself superior. When they feel secure, he will destroy many and take his stand against the Prince of princes (Daniel 8:24–25).

With flattery he will corrupt those who have violated the covenant, but the people who know their God will firmly resist him (Daniel 11:32).

The king will do as he pleases. He will exalt and magnify himself above every god and will say unheard-of things against the God of gods. He will be successful until the time of [God's] *wrath is completed* (Daniel 11:36).

Daniel has told us a great deal about this future world leader who will rise to power and then confirm a covenant with Israel. This covenant will ensure Israel's peace and security for three and a half years, until *"He"* (the Antichrist) turns against Israel.

The abomination that causes desolation

In this next part of Daniel's seventieth week prophecy, we see how the Antichrist will turn against Israel:

In the middle of the 'seven' he will put an end to sacrifice and offering. And on a wing of the temple he will set up an abomination that causes desolation (Daniel 9:27b).

In the middle of the seven-year period, or after three and a half years, the Antichrist will put an end to the Jewish practice of temple worship. At that time the Antichrist will also set himself up in the temple of God, saying that he is God. Daniel tells us about this again when he describes circumstances of the *abomination that causes desolation.*

> *His armed forces will rise up to desecrate the temple fortress and will abolish the daily sacrifice. Then they will set up the abomination that causes desolation. With flattery he will corrupt those who have violated the covenant, but the people who know their God will firmly resist him* (Daniel 11:31,32).

In order for the Antichrist to put an end to the practice of sacrifice and offering, the temple will first need to be rebuilt. Today, in 2003, there is no Jewish temple; nor is animal sacrifice and offering practiced in Jerusalem. Since A.D. 70, when the Roman general Titus destroyed Jerusalem and the temple, the Jewish people have had no temple. Since there is no place for the Jewish sacrifice and offering, the temple will need to be rebuilt before this prophecy can be fulfilled.

In these passages we see that the *abomination that causes desolation* will occur in the temple at the time the Antichrist stops sacrifice and offering. The *abomination that causes desolation* is the term given to the event that takes place when the Antichrist sets himself as God in the temple of God. Paul also described the *abomination that causes desolation* in his second letter to the Thessalonians (2 Thessalonians 2:4,5).

Recalling what Jesus told us in the Olivet Discourse, we know that immediately after the *abomination that causes desolation*, there will be a time of unprecedented persecution, which Jesus called the Great Tribulation (Matthew 24:21). We also know from Daniel's prophecy, and numerous others in Scripture, that the duration between the *abomination that causes desolation* and the end of the Great Tribulation will be "a time, times and half a time" (Daniel 7:25 and Revelation 12:14), or three and a half years.

■ THE GREAT TRIBULATION

Therefore, the Great Tribulation will start with the *abomination that causes desolation* and last three and a half years. Jesus described the Great Tribulation in very similar terms, as we have already seen in Matthew 24:21.

At that time Michael, the great prince who protects your people, will arise [amad]. *There will be a time of distress such as has not happened from the beginning of nations until then. But at that time your people—everyone whose name is found written in the book—will be delivered* (Daniel 12:1).

In this passage, Daniel tells us that after the archangel Michael arises, the Great Tribulation begins. The Hebrew word *amad* is translated "*arise.*" *Amad* also means to take one's stand and to rise up.[9] We will discover what Michael does when he takes his stand when we study 2 Thessalonians 2 and Revelation 12 later in the book.

Daniel also tells us that, at the time of the Great Tribulation, everyone whose name is found written in the book (of Life) will be delivered; many who sleep in the dust of the earth will awake. Scripture is clear that all believers have their names written in the book of life. The "*book of life*" is God's record of true believers; see the scriptural references to it below:

May they be blotted out of the book of life and not be listed with the righteous (Psalm 69:28).

Yes, and I ask you, loyal yokefellow, help these women who have contended at my side in the cause of the gospel, along with Clement and the rest of my fellow workers, whose names are in the book of life (Philemon 4:3).

If anyone's name was not found written in the book of life, he was thrown into the lake of fire (Revelation 20:15).

Therefore, we can safely say that following the Great Tribulation, all believers whose names are found written in the *book of life* will be delivered at the resurrection of the living and the dead. This conclusion is exactly what Jesus Christ explained to us when He answered the disciples' question about His return in Matthew 24:29–31.

Immediately after the distress of those days... They will see the Son of Man coming on the clouds of the sky, with power and great glory. And he will send his angels with a loud trumpet call, and they will gather his elect from the four winds, from one end of the heavens to the other (Matthew 24:29–31).

The end is poured out on him

As we have seen, the Great Tribulation will last three and a half years and will end when Christ returns on the "*great and dreadful day of the Lord.*" Let's see how Daniel records it as he closes this important prophecy—"*...until the end that is decreed is poured out on him* [Antichrist]" (Daniel 9:27d).

Daniel closes the Seventy Sevens prophecy by describing the end as being "poured out on" the Antichrist. The end of the age, as we have read in Jesus' teachings, is going to be a time of judgment and wrath on the unbelieving world. The Bible often describes the wrath of God as being "poured out," which we also see in Revelation when John describes what will happen to the Antichrist as the bowls of God's wrath are poured out on the beast (Antichrist) and his kingdom. *"The fifth angel poured out his bowl on the throne of the beast, and his kingdom was plunged into darkness"* (Revelation 16:10).

Daniel gives us additional information, regarding the final outcome of the Antichrist, in another vision; he tells us that the saints will inherit the Kingdom of God on earth.

> *But the court will sit, and his* [Antichrist] *power will be taken away and completely destroyed forever. Then the sovereignty, power and greatness of the kingdoms under the whole heaven will be handed over to the saints, the people of the Most High* (Daniel 7:26,27).

Thy Kingdom come on earth

Returning a moment to the first verse of Daniel's Seventy Sevens prophecy, we see that God will restore everything to the state before the fall of man when the Seventy Sevens are fulfilled.

> *Seventy 'sevens' are decreed for your people and your holy city to finish transgression, to put an end to sin, to atone for wickedness, to bring in everlasting righteousness, to seal up vision and prophecy and to anoint the most holy* (Daniel 9:24).

Daniel was given various visions regarding the restoration of all things when the Kingdom of God would be established on earth. Read how he saw the coming of the Kingdom of God on earth.

In the time of those kings, the God of heaven will set up a kingdom that will never be destroyed, nor will it be left to another people. It will crush all those kingdoms and bring them to an end, but it will itself endure forever (Daniel 2:44).

The four great beasts are four kingdoms that will rise from the earth. But the saints of the Most High will receive the kingdom and will possess it forever— yes, for ever and ever (Daniel 7:17,18).

Then the sovereignty, power and greatness of the kingdoms under the whole heaven will be handed over to the saints, the people of the Most High. His kingdom will be an everlasting kingdom, and all rulers will worship and obey him. 'This is the end of the matter...' (Daniel 7:27,28).

Finally, during Daniel's vision above he is told, *"This is the end of the matter"* (Daniel 7:28). This is the same expression Solomon used as he concluded his writings in Ecclesiastes:

Now all has been heard; here is the end of the matter: Fear God and keep his commandments, for this is the whole duty of man. For God will bring every deed into judgment, including every hidden thing, whether it is good or evil (Ecclesiastes 12:13,14).

Let's consider the wisdom of Solomon as we conclude our study of Daniel regarding the last days. Next, we will study Paul's writings, starting with 1 Corinthians 15.

CHAPTER FOUR

Listen, I Tell You a Mystery

Listen, I tell you a mystery:
We will not all sleep, but we will all
be changed—in a flash, in the twinkling
of an eye, at the last trumpet
(1 Corinthians 15:51,52).

Paul's first letter to the Corinthians gives us a comprehensive discourse on the resurrection of the believers. First, he assures us of the fact of Christ's resurrection, and then he explains the importance and purpose of Christ's resurrection for the believers.

> *But Christ has indeed been raised from the dead, the first fruits of those who have fallen asleep. For since death came through a man, the resurrection of the dead comes also through a man. For as in Adam all die, so in Christ all will be made alive. But each in his own turn: Christ, the first fruits; then, when he comes [parousia], those who belong to him* (1 Corinthians 15:20–23).

Here Paul explains the order of the resurrection of

believers. First Christ was resurrected from the dead, and
then, at Christ's return, all believers will be resurrected.
Since we have already studied the meaning of the Greek
word *parousia*, we recall that it signifies the arrival of Jesus
Christ to earth.

As Paul concludes his teaching on the resurrection of
believers, he tells us a mystery about the resurrection of
believers. Paul has previously defined what he means by the
term *"mystery"* in Ephesians 3:4–5. He says a mystery is
something which was previously not made known, but is
now revealed to the Church. This understanding of what
Paul means is further strengthened by a look back to the
Greek. The Greek word for "mystery" is *musterion*.
Musterion means "a secret, mystery (of something formerly
unknown but now revealed)."[1] Paul is revealing something
previously unknown. Therefore, the "mystery" must be
something not previously revealed. Let's study the Scripture
to see if we can determine what the mystery is. Read this
passage carefully to find the clues Paul provides.

> *Listen, I tell you a mystery: We will not all sleep, but
> we will all be changed—in a flash, in the twinkling
> of an eye, at the last trumpet. For the trumpet will
> sound, the dead will be raised imperishable, and we
> will be changed. For the perishable must clothe itself
> with the imperishable, and the mortal with immor-
> tality. When the perishable has been clothed with
> the imperishable, and the mortal with immortality,
> then the saying that is written will come true:
> "Death has been swallowed up in victory." Where,
> O death, is your victory? Where, O death, is your
> sting?* (1 Corinthians 15:51–55).

■ THE MYSTERY IS NOT THE RESURRECTION OF THE DEAD

The resurrection of the dead itself is not the mystery, because at the time of this letter, the resurrection of the dead had already been written about extensively. The resurrection is described in the Old Testament, taught by Christ Himself, and also previously taught by Paul in the letters to the Thessalonians. Let's examine some Old Testament prophecies first: *"Therefore my heart is glad and my tongue rejoices; my body also will rest secure, because you will not abandon me to the grave"* (Psalms 16:9, 10); *"But your dead will live; their bodies will rise. You, who dwell in the dust, wake up and shout for joy"* (Isaiah 26:19).

> *At that time Michael, the great prince who protects your people, will arise. There will be a time of distress such as has not happened from the beginning of nations until then. But at that time your people— everyone whose name is found written in the book—will be delivered. Multitudes who sleep in the dust of the earth will awake: some to everlasting life, others to shame and everlasting contempt* (Daniel 12:1,2).

> *I will ransom them from the power of the grave; I will redeem them from death. Where, O death, are your plagues? Where, O grave, is your destruction?* (Hosea 13:14).

The term *"resurrection"* was not actually used in the Old Testament. However, the prophets clearly describe for us how God's people will be raised from the dead. During His ministry, Jesus also taught regarding the resurrection of the righteous, which is recorded in all four Gospels.

Jesus replied, "You are in error because you do not know the Scriptures or the power of God. At the resurrection of believers people will neither marry nor be given in marriage; they will be like the angels in heaven" (Matthew 22:29,30).

"When the dead rise, they will neither marry nor be given in marriage; they will be like the angels in heaven" (Mark 12:25).

"...And you will be blessed. Although they cannot repay you, you will be repaid at the resurrection of the righteous" (Luke 14:14).

"For my Father's will is that everyone who looks to the Son and believes in him shall have eternal life, and I will raise him up at the last day" (John 6:40).

Since the Resurrection of the dead is well established in both the Old Testament and the teachings of Jesus, it is already known and, therefore, cannot be the mystery. What *is* the mystery? Let's look at the beginning of the passage again:

Listen, I tell you a mystery: We will not all sleep, but we will all be changed—in a flash, in the twinkling of an eye, at the last trumpet. For the trumpet will sound, the dead will be raised imperishable, and we will be changed (1 Corinthians 15:51,52).

■ THE MYSTERY IS NOT THE RESURRECTION OF THE LIVING

Paul reminds us that, at the resurrection of believers, all believers will be changed. First, he says that not all believers will sleep—which means not all believers will die. But, he then says, all believers will be changed—those that have died and those that are still alive—at the time of the resurrection.

By implication, Paul is saying that, at the time of the resurrection, some believers will still be alive. At this point, he goes on to indicate that the resurrection of all believers will take place in an instant. Paul explained how this would happen a few years earlier when he wrote his first letter to the Thessalonians. Let's see how he describes it:

> *According to the Lord's own word, we tell you that we who are still alive, who are left till the coming [parousia] of the Lord, will certainly not precede those who have fallen asleep. For the Lord himself will come down from heaven, with a loud command, with the voice of the archangel and with the trumpet call of God, and the dead in Christ will rise first. After that, we who are still alive and are left will be caught up together with them in the clouds to meet the Lord in the air* (1 Thessalonians 4:15–17).

Here Paul describes to us the catching up of living believers, those who are left alive, at the time of the resurrection. This "catching up" is what is commonly referred to as the Rapture. So, in 1 Corinthians 15, Paul is repeating what he has previously written in 1 Thessalonians 4: the dead and the living in Christ will be resurrected together.

Notice, in this passage, that Paul says, *"according to the Lord's own word… we who are still alive"* will also be gathered. Paul was apparently aware Jesus had taught that the living in Christ would also be changed at the time of the resurrection.

Paul may have been aware of the Lord's teaching as recorded in the Gospel of John. Jesus first told us, in His own words, that the living will also be changed in the resurrection, when He and Martha were discussing the resurrection following the death of her brother Lazarus.

John recorded the following conversation between Jesus and Martha:

> *Jesus said to her, "Your brother will rise again."*
> *Martha answered, "I know he will rise again in the*
> *resurrection at the last day." Jesus said to her, "I am*
> *the resurrection and the life. He who believes in me*
> *will live, even though he dies; and whoever lives and*
> *believes in me will never die. Do you believe this?"*
> (John 11:23–26).

Jesus was telling Martha that, in the resurrection of believers at the last day, those who had died would rise to life. He then went on to say that believers still alive at the last day would never die. This teaching reveals that at the last day, all believers will be resurrected together.

Jesus also described the resurrection of all believers when He said the angels would gather His elect—the living from earth and the dead from heaven. See the commentary on Matthew 24:31 in chapter 2, "According to the Lord's Own Word."

It is clear that Jesus taught that those alive in Christ will be part of the resurrection of believers and that Paul had previously taught this as well. Therefore, the mystery cannot be about who will be in the resurrection, because it was known that all believers, the living and the dead would be part of the resurrection.

■ WHAT IS THE MYSTERY?

There is, however, something else in this passage that Paul reveals, which had never been revealed in Scripture before he wrote it here. Let's re-examine the passage to see if we can identify what the real mystery is.

*Listen, I tell you a mystery: We will not all sleep, but
we will all be changed—in a flash, in the twinkling
of an eye, **at the last trumpet**. For the trumpet will
sound, the dead will be raised imperishable, and we
will be changed. For the perishable must clothe itself
with the imperishable, and the mortal with immortality. **When** the perishable has been clothed with
the imperishable, and the mortal with immortality,
then the saying that is written will come true:
"Death has been swallowed up in victory." Where,
O death, is your victory? Where, O death, is your
sting?* (1 Corinthians 15:51–55).

As we look carefully, we find there are three references
contained in the text that give indications of the timing of
the resurrection of believers. First, we see that the resurrection occurs "at the last trumpet." We have already studied
several Scripture verses where a trumpet sounds in connection with the resurrection of believers (1 Thessalonians
4:16; Matthew 24:31). However, this is the first time in
Scripture that the trumpet is identified as "*the last
trumpet.*" The Greek word *eschatos* is translated "last."
Thayer's Greek-English Lexicon of the New Testament
translates *eschatos* in this passage as "the trumpet after
which no other will sound."[2]

So, the mystery that Paul is describing could be that the
resurrection of believers will take place "*at the last
trumpet.*" This would be a very significant revelation
because, during the Jewish Feast of Trumpets, many trumpets are sounded. Also, as we will see when we study
Revelation, seven trumpets are described in relation to the
end times. The last trumpet we find in the biblical record is
the seventh trumpet, which is first mentioned in Revelation

10:7. Carefully compare this passage in Revelation to 1 Corinthians 15:51–52, and see the similarities:

But in the days when the seventh angel is about to sound his trumpet, the mystery of God will be accomplished, just as he announced to his servants the prophets (Revelation 10:7).

Listen, I tell you a mystery: We will not all sleep, but we will all be changed— in a flash, in the twinkling of an eye, at the last trumpet (1 Corinthians 15:51,52).

The similarities in these two passages are not coincidental. They both indicate that "the mystery" will be accomplished "*at the last* [seventh] *trumpet.*" Therefore, if "the last trumpet" is the "*seventh trumpet*" of Revelation, we would expect to see evidence that the resurrection of believers will take place when the seventh trumpet sounds. When we examine Revelation 11:15–18, we see several things taking place when the seventh trumpet sounds:

The seventh angel sounded his trumpet, and there were loud voices in heaven, which said: "The kingdom of the world has become the kingdom of our Lord and of his Christ, and he will reign for ever and ever." "You have taken your great power and begun to reign. The nations were angry and your wrath has come. The time has come for judging the dead, and for rewarding your servants the prophets and your saints and those who reverence your name, both small and great—and for destroying those who destroy the earth" (Revelation 11:15–18).

When the seventh trumpet sounds, we first see that the Lord has established His Kingdom on earth. Next, John tells us that the nations are angry and the wrath of God has come. The wrath of God, as we know, occurs on the Day of the Lord, as revealed throughout Scripture; see Isaiah 13:9 and Zephaniah 1:14–15 for examples.

John tells us next that it is time to judge and reward all the believers. In order to judge the believers, the Bible clearly states that they must first be resurrected and gathered; see Psalm 50:4–5. Therefore, John describes for us the resurrection of all believers at the seventh and last trumpet. This is confirmation that the resurrection of believers occurs at *"the last trumpet,"* just as Paul prophesied in 1 Corinthians 15:51,52.

While this seems to be conclusive evidence that the resurrection of all believers takes place at *"the last trumpet,"* some may ask for more. For those, notice that there are two additional time indicators in 1 Corinthians 15:51–55. Paul says,

> **When** *the perishable has been clothed with the imperishable, and the mortal with immortality,* **then** *the saying that is written will come true: "Death has been swallowed up in victory." Where, O death, is your victory? Where, O death, is your sting?* (1 Corinthians 15:54,55).

To paraphrase, Paul tells us that *when* we have been changed, *then* death will be defeated. Paul is connecting the timing mystery to passages in the Old Testament that foretell the victory over death. The two clearest connections are in Isaiah 25:8 and Hosea 13:14. Paul is confirming the timing of the resurrection as the mystery when he makes reference to these expressions. First, let's look at Isaiah's prophecy:

> *On this mountain the* LORD *Almighty will prepare a feast of rich food for all peoples, a banquet of aged*

*wine—the best of meats and the finest of wines. On this mountain he will destroy the shroud that enfolds all peoples, the sheet that covers all nations; **he will swallow up death forever.** The Sovereign* LORD *will wipe away the tears from all faces; he will remove the disgrace of his people from all the earth. The* LORD *has spoken. In that day they will say, Surely this is our God; we trusted in him, and he saved us. This is the* LORD, *we trusted in him; let us rejoice and be glad in his salvation. The hand of the* LORD *will rest on this mountain* (Isaiah 25:6–10).

This beautifully descriptive passage in Isaiah opens with the Lord preparing what can only be the wedding feast between Christ and His bride, the Church. The Lord has returned and established the Kingdom of God on earth. Isaiah says "*in that day,*" when Jesus returns to earth, "*death has been swallowed up in victory,*" which is a change that occurs in our bodies at the resurrection. See how Jesus describes this:

"But those who are considered worthy of taking part in that age and in the resurrection from the dead will neither marry nor be given in marriage, and they can no longer die; for they are like the angels. They are God's children, since they are children of the resurrection" (Luke 20:35,36).

These are characteristics of what will happen when Jesus returns on the Day of the Lord to establish the Kingdom on earth.

The wording in Hosea is slightly different from Isaiah, but it is equally descriptive of the victory over death which occurs at the resurrection.

> *I will ransom them from the power of the grave; I will redeem them from death.* **Where, O death, are your plagues?** *Where, O grave, is your destruction?* (Hosea 13:14).

At the resurrection of believers, death will have been defeated. Both Isaiah and Hosea describe this as happening at the restoration of Israel when Christ establishes the Kingdom of God on earth.

In Revelation, at the seventh trumpet, we see the resurrection occurring at the time that the Kingdom is established on earth. In Isaiah and Hosea, we see the same thing—the resurrection occurs at the time that the Kingdom is established on earth. Therefore, when Paul wrote, "*Listen, I tell you a mystery,*" he was revealing the timing of the resurrection of the living and the dead. The resurrection of believers will take place at the last trumpet, when Christ returns to establish the Kingdom of God on earth.

So far in our study, through the teachings of Christ, the prophecies of Daniel and now the writings of Paul, we have seen a clear and consistent picture: the resurrection of all believers will take place after the Great Tribulation, when Jesus returns to establish the Kingdom of God on earth, on the Day of the Lord.

Now, let's look at Paul's first letter to the Thessalonians where he is trying to clear up some confusion with regard to the return of the Lord and the gathering of the Church.

CHAPTER FIVE

Brothers, We Do Not Want You to Be Ignorant

Brothers, we do not want you to be ignorant about those who fall asleep, or to grieve like the rest of men, who have no hope (1 Thessalonians 4:13).

Paul's letters to the Thessalonians predated his letters to the Corinthians by several years. Paul was only in Thessalonica for about a month before he was forced to leave because of severe persecution. A month with the new believers in Thessalonica was probably too short a time to adequately cover the elementary teachings of the gospel, which Paul called "*spiritual milk.*" Soon there developed confusion regarding the resurrection of believers and the Day of the Lord. In Paul's first letter, he addresses their concerns about those who have died in Christ and explains that they, too, will be gathered with the living at Christ's return. Paul also reassures them that the Day of the Lord will not take them by surprise, as it will the unbelieving world. In this letter to the Thessalonians, Paul provides us with important insights into the return of the Lord and the end

of the age. We will now look at excerpts from his first letter
to the Thessalonians.

■ 1 THESSALONIANS 1

In chapter one, Paul commends the Thessalonian
church for their faith and encourages them as they wait for
Jesus Christ, who will come down from heaven and rescue
them from the coming wrath of God: *"wait for his Son from
heaven, whom he raised from the dead—Jesus, who rescues
us from the coming wrath"* (1 Thessalonians 1:10).

■ 1 THESSALONIANS 2

Paul continues his encouragement as he tells the church
that their hope, their joy and crown will come when they
glory in the presence of their Lord at His arrival. *"For what
is our hope, our joy, or the crown in which we will glory in
the presence of our Lord Jesus when he comes?* [parousia]"
(1 Thessalonians 2:19).

"The crown" is a symbol of our reward, which we will
receive at the Judgment Seat of Christ when He returns
from heaven. Notice that once again, Paul uses the Greek
word *parousia*, signifying Christ's arrival. In Paul's letter to
Titus, he again tells us that our hope is in Christ at His
appearing: *"while we wait for the blessed hope—the glorious appearing* [epiphaneia] *of our great God and Savior,
Jesus Christ"* (Titus 2:13).

The Greek word *epiphaneia* is translated *"appearing"*
and means a manifestation, i.e. (specifically) the Advent of
Christ (past or future):—appearing, brightness.[1] Note that
the Greek words *parousia* and *epiphaneia* are both used by
Paul to express the physical and visible return of Christ.
Paul makes it clear that our hope is in Christ. This blessed
hope brings our deliverance, resurrection and reward.

■ 1 Thessalonians 3

Paul encourages the Church to remain strong and persevere as we wait for the arrival of the Lord with His holy ones.

May he strengthen your hearts so that you will be blameless and holy in the presence of our God and Father when our Lord Jesus comes [parousia] *with all his holy ones* (1 Thessalonians 3:13).

The "holy ones" in this context are most likely the angels which, as we have seen in Matthew 13:39 and Matthew 24:30–31, will gather all believers during the *harvest*. In Paul's second letter to the Thessalonians, he again refers to the angels as coming with the Lord when Christ is revealed from heaven.

...and give relief to you who are troubled and to us as well. This will happen when the Lord Jesus is revealed [apokalupsis] *from heaven in blazing fire with his powerful angels* (2 Thessalonians 1:7).

The Greek word *apokalupsis* is translated "revealed" in this verse. *Apokalupsis* means to be revealed, revealing, revelation.[2] We now have seen that Paul uses three different Greek words to signify the physical and visible return of Jesus Christ. He uses *parousia* most often, but he also uses the Greek words *epiphaneia* and *apokalupsis* interchangeably as he describes the coming of the Lord with His mighty angels.

■ 1 Thessalonians 4

One of the main issues Paul addresses in this letter concerns those who have fallen asleep in Christ. Apparently the Thessalonians were not aware that those who died in Christ would also participate in the resurrection at Jesus' return on the Day of the Lord. Paul reassures them that all believers, both living and dead, will be gathered together, and that we will all meet the Lord in the air when Christ comes down from heaven. Let's examine carefully this key passage on the resurrection of believers:

> *Brothers, we do not want you to be ignorant about those who fall asleep, or to grieve like the rest of men, who have no hope. We believe that Jesus died and rose again and so we believe that God will bring with Jesus those who have fallen asleep in him. According to the Lord's own word, we tell you that we who are still alive, who are left till the coming [parousia] of the Lord, will certainly not precede those who have fallen asleep. For the Lord himself will come down from heaven, with a loud command, with the voice of the archangel and with the trumpet call of God, and the dead in Christ will rise first. After that, we who are still alive and are left will be caught up together with them in the clouds to meet [apentesis] the Lord in the air. And so we will be with the Lord forever. Therefore encourage each other with these words* (1 Thessalonians 4:13–18).

This passage vividly describes that the dead in Christ will be gathered together in the clouds with those who are still alive at the arrival of the Lord. Believers who are alive at that time will be caught up ("raptured") as they are gathered together to meet the Lord in the air. We examined this passage briefly when we studied the mystery of the last trumpet; however, I will make a few additional observations.

Paul reassures the Thessalonians that those who have died will not be left out as he explains that the resurrection of the living and the dead will take place at the same time.

In detailing the specific steps of the resurrection of believers, the apostle says that the dead in Christ will rise first, and then *"we who are still alive and are left will be caught up together with them to meet the Lord in the air."* In effect there seems to be no time difference between the catching up of the living and the gathering of the dead in Christ. The dead and the living are gathered together in the clouds. In 1 Corinthians 15:51,52, Paul says, *"we will all be changed— in a flash, in the twinkling of an eye."* Therefore, it appears from what is written that the living and the dead in Christ will be changed in the resurrection so quickly that any difference in the timing will be indistinguishable.

The Lord comes down from heaven

In verse 16, Paul says the Lord will come down from heaven to gather together the church. When the Lord left the earth at the end of His First Advent, He returned to heaven where He sits at the right hand of God the Father. He will remain in Heaven until it is time for Him to return to earth and set up the Kingdom of God. When He returns, he will come down from heaven with His angels, just as prophesied in Scripture. Here are a few Old Testament passages that provide a clear picture of the event.

> *"Shout and be glad, O Daughter of Zion. For I am coming, and I will live among you,"* declares the LORD... *Be still before the* LORD, *all mankind, because he has roused himself from his holy dwelling* (Zechariah 2:10, 13).

> *"Part your heavens, O Lord, and come down; touch the mountains, so that they smoke"* (Psalm 144:5).
> *"...so the Lord Almighty will come down to do battle on Mount Zion and on its heights"* (Isaiah 31:4).

"Look! The Lord is coming from his dwelling place; he comes down and treads the high places of the earth" (Micah 1:3).

We also find references to His coming down out of heaven as recorded by the apostles of the New Testament:

"He must remain in heaven until the time comes for God to restore everything, as he promised long ago through his holy prophets" (Acts 3:21).

"This will happen when the Lord Jesus is revealed from heaven in blazing fire with his powerful angels" (2 Thessalonians 1:7).

As we examine these verses, we see that when the Lord returns to restore everything and establish the Kingdom on earth, he will leave heaven and return to earth.

With a loud command and trumpet call

In verse 16, Paul tells us that the Lord will come down from heaven with *"a loud command, with the voice of the archangel and with the trumpet call of God."* The loud command most likely will come from Christ because, in the Gospel of John, we are told we will hear the voice of God in relation to the resurrection:

> *I tell you the truth, a time is coming and has now come when the dead will hear the voice of the Son of God and those who hear will live... Do not be amazed at this, for a time is coming when all who are in their graves will hear his voice and come out—those who have done good will rise to live, and those who have done evil will rise to be condemned* (John 5:25–29).

As for the trumpet call, we have already studied this in our examination of Matthew 24:31 and 1 Corinthians 15:51,52. The trumpet call of God is the well-established signal found throughout Scripture in connection with the coming of the Lord. As we study the return of Christ, we find that the trumpet call is the signal for the gathering of His chosen ones. The following verses represent a sample of Scripture on the topic. *"Then the LORD will appear over them; his arrow will flash like lightning. The Sovereign LORD will sound the trumpet"* (Zechariah 9:14); *"And he will send his angels with a loud trumpet call, and they will gather his elect from the four winds, from one end of the heavens to the other"* (Matthew 24:31).

We will be with the Lord forever

In verse 17, Paul says, *"and so we will be with the Lord forever,"* telling us that from the time of Christ's return, the saints will be with Him. Christ tells us the same thing, as recorded in the Gospel of John:

> *"In my Father's house are many rooms; if it were not so, I would have told you. I am going there to prepare a place for you. And if I go and prepare a place for you, I will come back and take you to be with me that you also may be where I am"* (John 14:2,3).

Let's now summarize the key points from 1 Thessalonians 4:13–18. We have identified the following four aspects of the resurrection at the return of Christ:

1. The Lord Jesus Christ will come down from heaven.
2. The Lord will come with a loud command, with the voice of the archangel and the trumpet call.
3. At the resurrection of the believers, the living and the dead will be gathered together.
4. After the resurrection, all believers will be with the Lord forever.

John F. Walvoord, who promoted the Pre-Tribulation Rapture Theory, said in his book, *End Times*, "The major passage on the Rapture is 1 Thessalonians 4:13–18."[3] Since 1 Thessalonians 4:13–18 is considered the major passage for the Pre-Tribulation Rapture Theory, we should expect to find support for that theory in that passage.

While the passage is a clear picture of the Rapture, there is no reference to when the Rapture will happen. There is no mention of Daniel's seventieth week, the Great Tribulation or the time of the Antichrist. Since there is no indication of timing, this passage cannot provide support for a Pre-Tribulation Rapture.

It's Greek to us

There are, however, other methods we can employ to examine this passage to gain understanding of God's plan. The first method is to look to the Greek text from which the passage was translated. As we have seen before, studying the Greek can often help us gain insight and understanding into the true meaning of the passage.

Parousia

We have already studied the Greek word *parousia* and we realize it means the arrival, or the physical and visible return, of our Lord Jesus Christ to earth. An additional insight into the word *parousia* will help us gain a deeper understanding to its meaning. First, let's look at the passage again:

> *According to the Lord's own word, we tell you that we who are still alive, who are left till the coming [parousia] of the Lord, will certainly not precede those who have fallen asleep. For the Lord himself will come down from heaven, with a loud command, with*

the voice of the archangel and with the trumpet call of
God, and the dead in Christ will rise first. After that,
we who are still alive and are left will be caught up
together with them in the clouds to meet [apentesis]
the Lord in the air (1 Thessalonians 4:15–17).

Another view of the Greek word *parousia,* as it is used
in the New Testament, will help our understanding of this
passage. According to the writers of *Vocabulary of the
Greek Testament:*

> What, however, more especially concerns us in con-
> nection with the NT usage of "parousia" is the
> quasi-technical force of the word from Ptolemaic
> times onwards to denote the "visit" of a King,
> Emperor, or other person in authority, the official
> character of the "visit" being further emphasized by
> the taxes or payments that were exacted to make
> preparation for it.[4]

As we can see from the *Vocabulary of the Greek
Testament,* not only does the word *parousia* signify the event
of an arrival, but at that time in history, *parousia* was used to
indicate the arrival of a king or a person in authority. This, of
course, is exactly what Paul tells us in this passage. Here
parousia indicates the arrival of Jesus Christ, the King of
kings, as He returns to establish His Kingdom on earth.

Apantesis

Another Greek word in this passage will also help us
correctly understand what Paul is saying. The Greek word
apantesis is translated as "meet." *Apantesis* has a specific
application and technical meaning. "The word *apantesis*
seems to have been a kind of official welcome of a newly

arriving dignitary—a usage which accords excellently with its NT usage."[5] As a matter of fact, the meaning of *apantesis* is so special that it is used just four times in the entire Bible. Three of the four times it is used are in connection with the return of Christ—twice in the Gospel of Matthew and once here in 1 Thessalonians 4:17. First, let's look at how *apantesis* is used in the Olivet Discourse:

> *"At that time the Kingdom of heaven will be like ten virgins who took their lamps and went out to meet* [apantesis] *the bridegroom... At midnight the cry rang out: Here's the bridegroom! Come out to meet* [apantesis] *him!"* (Matthew 25:1,6).

Here, in the Parable of the Ten Virgins, the virgins go out to meet the approaching bridegroom to join him as He arrives for the wedding banquet. This is the very same event being described by Paul in 1 Thessalonians 4:17. The believers are represented by the five wise virgins who will go out to meet the Lord and then continue with Him to the wedding banquet. In both passages, Jesus is on His way to the wedding feast on Mount Zion in Jerusalem; see Isaiah 25:6–8.

Apantesis is used on only one other occasion in Scripture, in Acts, when Luke describes the meeting between the believers from Rome and Paul as he arrives on the outskirts of the city. They meet him and continue with him to Rome.

> *The brothers there had heard that we were coming, and they traveled as far as the Forum of Appius and the Three Taverns to meet* [apantesis] *us. At the sight of these men Paul thanked God and was encouraged* (Acts 28:15).

Therefore, each of the four uses of *apantesis* in Scripture are consistent with the meaning in 1 Thessalonians 4:17.

While we are not directly told the timing of Christ's return, it should be clear that Paul describes Christ's return as the King of kings. Christ is coming to earth to hold the wedding feast and establish the Kingdom on earth, which is exactly what Jesus described in the Parable of the Ten Virgins.

Context, context, context

One more test can be applied to this passage, which further confirms that the resurrection of believers will occur after the Great Tribulation. Since 1 Thessalonians 4:13–18 does not directly reveal the timing of the resurrection of believers, we must look to the rest of Paul's letter to determine if the timing is indicated in its context. Our understanding must be guided by following the three rules of proper interpretation: "Context, Context and Context."

As we look at the entire letter, we find that the return of Christ is mentioned in all five chapters. In chapter one, Jesus returns from heaven to rescue us from the coming wrath, placing His return and our rescue at the end of the Great Tribulation and the seven bowls of God's wrath.[6] In chapter two, the arrival [*parousia*] of the Lord is connected with the receiving of our crowns, which we receive at our judgment (Revelation 11:18). In Thessalonians 2, 3 and 4, the Greek word *parousia* is used in reference to the arrival of the Lord. Paul's use of the Greek word *parousia* is strong evidence for the position that his whole letter refers to the arrival of Christ at the end of the age.

■ 1 THESSALONIANS 5

In the final chapter, we gain even more confirmation into the timing of the return of Jesus Christ. Once again Paul connects the return of Christ with the Day of the Lord.

No surprise for believers!

Paul tells us that the coming of the Lord will not surprise the true believers, but it will catch the unbelieving world off guard:

> *Now, brothers, about times and dates we do not need to write to you, for you know very well that the day of the Lord will come like a thief in the night. While **people** are saying, "Peace and safety," destruction will come on **them** suddenly, as labor pains on a pregnant woman, and **they** will not escape. But you, brothers, are not in darkness so that this day should surprise you like a thief. You are all sons of the light and sons of the day. We do not belong to the night or to the darkness* (1 Thessalonians 5:1–5).

Paul first reminds the Thessalonians that he has already instructed them about the timing of the Day of the Lord. He tells them "*the Day of the Lord will come like a thief in the night.*" It is very important that we are clear about this expression. Many people mistakenly think that believers cannot know the general time of Christ's return. However, just because Paul is writing this *to* the Church does not mean he is writing this *about* the Church. This is written about the unbelievers, not the believers.

Look carefully at what Paul has written. When he says, "*the Day of the Lord will come like a thief in the night,*" he is referring to "*people,*" "*them,*" and "*they;*" Paul is making a distinction between the believers and the unbelievers. Consider what Paul says to the believers in verse four—"*But you, brothers, are not in darkness so that this day should surprise you like a thief.*" He is telling them that the Day of the Lord **will not** come on believers like a thief, because they are sons of the light. On the other hand, it will surprise the unbelieving world.

Jesus said the same thing, in Matthew 24:37, when He told us it will be *"as it was in the days of Noah"* before the Day of the Lord.

Tribulation is tribulation

Let's look at I Thessalonians 5 as Paul reassures us that God has not appointed us to suffer His wrath. *"For God did not appoint us to suffer wrath but to receive salvation through our Lord Jesus Christ"* (1 Thessalonians 5:9). God Himself will rescue us from His coming wrath. This is a spiritual principle that is well established throughout Scripture. The people of God have never come under the wrath of God—recall Sodom, Gomorrah and the Flood. God repeatedly assures us that we will not suffer His wrath when it comes on the Day of the Lord.

There is a spiritual principle in Scripture which we need to understand. The principle is that believers will suffer tribulation, distress and persecution and even physical death. Jesus clearly tells us that we will be persecuted when He says, *"if they persecuted me, they will persecute you also"* (John 15:20).

It has become popular, in these last days, to confuse tribulation with wrath and treat them as the same thing. Jesus has told us that after the Great Tribulation, He will appear in the clouds of the sky and gather His elect (Matthew 24:29–31). C.I. Scofield, in his popular study Bible, says Jesus will come before Daniel's seventieth week and the Great Tribulation.[7] His theory places the Wrath of God during the Tribulation. Simply stated, what Jesus says is Tribulation (Matthew 24:15–29), Scofield says is the wrath of God. Once again, if we hope to have a correct understanding of the Word of Truth, we must not go beyond what is written. When Jesus says Tribulation, He *means* Tribulation—not something else.

There is only one Second Coming of Christ, and it occurs on the Day of the Lord. Each of the five chapters of this letter refer to this one event. Compare these two passages to see the similarities:

> *After that, we who are still alive and are left will be caught up together with them in the clouds to meet the Lord in the air.* **And so we will be with the Lord forever.** *Therefore encourage each other with these words* (1 Thessalonians 4:17, 18).

> *He died for us so that,* **whether we are awake or asleep, we may live together with him.** *Therefore encourage one another and build each other up, just as in fact you are doing* (1 Thessalonians 5:10,11).

It should be clear: Paul is writing about the same thing in each of these passages. Would Paul use such similar language to describe two different events? *No!* The Bible is clear that there is only one Second Coming of Christ. It occurs immediately after the Great Tribulation on the Day of the Lord. Therefore,

> *May God himself, the God of peace, sanctify you through and through. May your whole spirit, soul and body be kept blameless at the coming* [parousia] *of our Lord Jesus Christ* (1 Thessalonians 5:23).

CHAPTER SIX

Don't Let Anyone Deceive You in Any Way

> *Don't let anyone deceive you in any way, for that day will not come until the rebellion occurs and the man of lawlessness is revealed, the man doomed to destruction.* (2 Thessalonians 2:3)

In Paul's second letter to the Thessalonians, he instructs them once again regarding the return of Christ and the Day of the Lord. In both letters to the Thessalonians Paul covers material he had previously taught them. In the second letter it appears that Paul is making absolutely sure they understand about the coming of Jesus Christ and our gathering on the Day of the Lord. Let's see how he makes it clear to the Church.

■ 2 THESSALONIANS 1

First, Paul gives a concise description of the events that will transpire when Christ returns. Let's look carefully at this passage to understand what Paul is telling us:

> *God is just: He will pay back trouble to those who trouble you and give relief to you who are troubled,*

*and to us as well. **This will happen when the Lord Jesus is revealed** (apokalupsis) from heaven in blazing fire with his powerful angels. He will punish those who do not know God and do not obey the gospel of our Lord Jesus. They will be punished with everlasting destruction and shut out from the presence of the Lord and from the majesty of his power **on the day he comes to be glorified** in his holy people and to be marveled at among all those who have believed. This includes you, because you believed our testimony to you* (2 Thessalonians 1:6–10).

Paul says when the Lord is revealed from heaven, He will give us relief from—and, at the same time, pay back those responsible for—our trouble. This relief is our deliverance, which Paul called *"the blessed hope"* of the Church, in Titus 2:13. The punishment *"with everlasting destruction"* is the wrath of God, which will be poured out on the unbelieving world on *"the day of reckoning"* (Isaiah 10:3). Therefore, when Paul says that our relief comes at the same time of God's judgment, he is telling us that the resurrection of believers and the wrath of God will both take place on the Day of the Lord.

Paul uses the Greek word *apokalupsis* to signify Christ's visible return to earth, just as he did in 1 Corinthians:

*Therefore you do not lack any spiritual gift as you eagerly wait for our **Lord Jesus Christ to be revealed** [apokalupsis]. He will keep you strong to the end, so that you will be blameless **on the day of our Lord Jesus Christ*** (1 Corinthians 1:7,8).

In both passages Paul says we are to wait for our deliverance until Jesus' return, on the Day of the Lord.

He comes to be glorified

Paul tells us that this will occur "*on the day he comes to be glorified.*" Once again we see a clear connection between the Day of the Lord and the coming of Christ. Both Isaiah and Zechariah also make this point abundantly clear in their prophecies regarding that day when the Lord alone will be exalted over the whole earth: "*The eyes of the arrogant man will be humbled and the pride of men brought low; the LORD alone will be exalted in that day*" (Isaiah 2:11); "*The LORD will be king over the whole earth. On that day there will be one LORD, and his name the only name*" (Zechariah 14:9).

If only Christ will be exalted over the whole earth on the Day of the Lord, that day must come after the Great Tribulation. For we know that during the Great Tribulation, the Antichrist will reign on the earth and he will be worshiped by the whole unbelieving world. So, if the Bible says Christ alone is exalted on the Day of the Lord, can the Antichrist be exalted at the same time? Those who hold to the opinion that the Day of the Lord comes before the end of the Great Tribulation would be wise to consider these verses.

Let's summarize what Paul has been saying in 2 Thessalonians 1:6–10. When Christ is revealed on the Day of the Lord:

- He will be revealed from heaven with His angels;
- He will give relief to the Church;
- He will punish the unbelievers;
- He will be glorified.

■ 2 THESSALONIANS 2—DON'T LET ANYONE DECEIVE YOU

In chapter two, Paul warns us that deception about the last days will come in many ways, even from seemingly reliable sources. His advice echoes the warnings Jesus gave during the Olivet Discourse. Paul is very concerned about the deception that had already slipped into the Thessalonian church. Apparently someone had introduced into the church—by letter or prophecy—a report saying that the Day of the Lord had already come. Let's look at how Paul tries to clear up the deception:

> **Concerning the coming** [parousia] **of our Lord Jesus Christ and our being gathered to him,** *we ask you, brothers, not to become easily unsettled or alarmed by some prophecy, report or letter supposed to have come from us, saying that the day of the Lord has already come. Don't let anyone deceive you in any way, for* **that day will not come until** *the rebellion* [apostasia] *occurs and the* **man of lawlessness is revealed,** *the man doomed to destruction. He will oppose and will exalt himself over everything that is called God or is worshiped, so that he sets himself up in God's temple, proclaiming himself to be God. Don't you remember that when I was with you I used to tell you these things?* (2 Thessalonians 2:1–5).

Paul warns us against any teaching not consistent with the gospel he proclaims. We find that, some years later, Paul also warned Timothy about Hymenaeus' and Philetus' teaching that *"the resurrection has already taken place"*:

> *Their teaching will spread like gangrene. Among them are Hymenaeus and Philetus, who have wandered away from the truth. They say that the resurrection has already taken place, and they destroy the faith of some* (2 Timothy 2:17,18).

The instructions in these passages provide an extremely important message that incorrectly handling the Word may result in separation from the truth and cause people to lose faith. Paul tells us that we must rely on the Word of God and not believe everything we hear.

Concerning the Coming of the Lord and our being gathered

Paul makes it absolutely clear that he is writing *"Concerning the coming of our Lord Jesus Christ and our being gathered to him."* This coming [*parousia*] is the same coming Paul wrote about in 1 Thessalonians 4:15. It is also the same coming [*parousia*] that Jesus describes in Matthew 24:3,27,37 and 39. In each of these passages, the Greek word *parousia* is used to identify the future Advent of Christ. **Paul also ties together Christ's coming, our gathering and the Day of the Lord. Therefore, Paul is telling us that the believers will be gathered when Christ returns on the Day of the Lord.** Paul goes on to say that the Day of the Lord will not come until after two things happen: *"the rebellion"* and the revealing of the *"man of lawlessness,"* the Antichrist.

After the rebellion!

The Greek word *apostasia* is translated in this passage as *"rebellion."* *Apostasia* means *"a falling away, defecting, apostasy."*[1] The English word *apostasy* is derived from *apostasia* and captures the meaning in the text. Apostasy means *"an abandoning of what one has believed in, as a faith."*[2]

Paul writes that the rebellion (falling away from the faith) will take place before Jesus returns and gathers the Church. We know from Matthew 24:9,10 that a time of worldwide persecution and death will take place in the future when many of the followers of Christ will turn away from the faith.

Jesus also warned us that there will be a time of great deception when *"false Christs and false prophets will appear and perform great signs and miracles to deceive even the elect—if that were possible*" (Matthew 24:24). Jesus is describing the circumstances which will take place during the Great Tribulation in both of these passages. The Great Tribulation is characterized in Scripture as a time of testing and "*trial that will come on the whole world*" (Revelation 3:10). During this time of tribulation and persecution, the turning away from the faith will occur as the followers of Christ are put to the ultimate test of their faith. Both Paul and Christ warn us about this time and alert us to this future falling away from the faith.

After the Antichrist is revealed!

Paul also tells us the Antichrist will be revealed before Jesus Christ returns. He goes on to describe the circumstances of the Antichrist's being revealed. The Antichrist "*sets himself up in God's temple, proclaiming himself to be God*" (2 Thessalonians 2:4). This will be the event called the *abomination that causes desolation*. We have already studied this in Daniel's prophecies and in the Olivet Discourse. Paul and Daniel both describe the Antichrist and the circumstances of the *abomination that causes desolation* in similar ways. Compare Paul's writing with Daniel's below and see the similarities.

> *He will oppose and **will exalt himself over everything that is called God** or is worshiped, so that **he sets himself up in God's temple**, proclaiming himself to be God.* (2 Thessalonians 2:4).

> *He will exalt and magnify himself above every god and will say unheard-of things against the God of gods* (Daniel 11:36).

> *His armed forces will rise up to desecrate **the temple***
> ***fortress** and will abolish the daily sacrifice. Then*
> *they will **set up the abomination that causes deso-***
> ***lation** (Daniel 11:31).*

> *He will confirm a covenant with many for one*
> *'seven.' In the middle of the 'seven' he will put an*
> *end to sacrifice and offering. And **on a wing of the***
> ***temple he will set up an abomination that causes***
> ***desolation**, until the end that is decreed is poured*
> *out on him (Daniel 9:27).*

The prophecies of Daniel 9:27 regarding the Antichrist match perfectly with Paul's prophecy about "*the man of lawlessness*" who will enter the temple of God and declare himself to be God. Therefore, we can determine what events must come before Christ's return:

- Antichrist will be revealed at the *abomination that causes desolation* (in the middle of Daniel's seventieth week).
- The turning away from the faith (during the Great Tribulation).

Then, after these two events, Christ will return on the Day of the Lord to gather the elect.

Antichrist will be revealed at the proper time

Paul goes on to tell us that the Antichrist will be revealed at the appointed time: "*And now you know what is holding him back, so that he* [Antichrist] *may be revealed at the proper time*" (2 Thessalonians 2:6).

Connecting the prophecies of Daniel with Paul's prophecies, we see that the Antichrist will be revealed at the *abomination that causes desolation.* We also know from Daniel and Jesus that the *abomination that causes desolation* occurs immediately before the Great Tribulation.

Now we are about to dig into one of the most fascinating, and perhaps challenging, eschatological mysteries of our study. Paul tells us that someone is *now* restraining *"the secret power of lawlessness."* He goes on to say that when he is no longer restraining *"the secret power of lawlessness"* the Antichrist will be revealed.

Who is *now* holding back the secret power of lawlessness? Let's look carefully at what Paul is telling us:

> *And now you know what is holding him back, so that he may be revealed at the proper time. For the secret power of lawlessness is already at work; but the one who **now** holds it back will continue to do so till he is taken out of the way. And then the lawless one will be revealed* (2 Thessalonians 2:6–8).

For centuries students and scholars alike have attempted to guess who the restrainer is—*"the one who **now** holds it back."* However, few seem to have consulted the Scriptures for the answer. One premise of our study is that if God desires us to know and understand a prophecy before it happens, He will provide the answer in Scripture. That is why we have repeatedly sought to have Scripture interpret Scripture for our understanding. The answer, if available, will be revealed by studying all Scripture related to the question. However, before we search for the identity of the restrainer, *"the one who **now** holds it back,"* we will first search for the identity of who is being held back. Paul indicates that there are three players in this last days scenario, and one we already know is the Antichrist.

1. He who is being held back   -   ?
2. He who is doing the holding   -   ?
3. He who will be revealed   -   **Antichrist**

Therefore, who is it that has the "*secret power of lawlessness*" which is being held back?

Who has the secret power of lawlessness?

What do we know about the one who has "*the secret power of lawlessness*"—other than that he is being held back? Paul says that "*the secret power of lawlessness*" is already at work, and the one who has it is currently being held back. Therefore, we know that in A.D. 51, when Paul wrote this letter, "*the secret power of lawlessness*" was already at work, and that he who has it was still being held back at that time. We also know that he will be held back until the time of the *abomination that causes desolation*, which is when the Antichrist will be revealed. Paul says,

> *He will oppose and will exalt himself over everything that is called God or is worshiped, so that he sets himself up in God's temple, proclaiming himself to be God... And now you know what is holding him back, so that he may be revealed at the proper time* (2 Thessalonians 2:4,6).

The Apostle John provides evidence to the identity of the one who has "*the secret power of lawlessness*" when he defines lawlessness. He then connects lawlessness to Satan. Notice that, like Paul, John also indicates that Satan has been at work from the beginning and is still at work even to this day: "*Everyone who sins breaks the law; in fact, sin is lawlessness*" (1 John 3:4); "*He who does what is sinful is of the devil, because the devil has been sinning from the beginning"* (1 John 3:8).

In these verses John defines "*sin*" as lawlessness and says that Satan is the power behind sin. While it seems clear that John is saying that Satan is the one who has the power of lawlessness, we should search further to determine if there is other Scripture to support this position. Let's look in the prophecies of Daniel and Revelation during the time of the Antichrist and the *abomination that causes desolation*, because Paul tells us the Antichrist will be revealed when Satan is no longer restrained. Are there any connections between Satan and the Antichrist? Let's look at some verses:

> *He* [Antichrist] *will become very strong, but **not by his own power**. He will cause astounding devastation and will succeed in whatever he does. He will destroy the mighty men and the holy people. He will cause deceit to prosper, and he will consider himself superior* (Daniel 8:24,25).

Daniel says the Antichrist will become very powerful but someone else will provide the power he needs. A characteristic of this power, which is evident in both Paul's and Daniel's writing, is deception; the Antichrist uses deception to mislead the world. "*He will cause deceit to prosper*" (Daniel 8:25) as he "*deceives those who are perishing*" (2 Thessalonians 2:10). Also, in Revelation, we see that Satan will give his power and authority to the Antichrist: "*The dragon* [Satan] *gave the beast* [Antichrist] *his power and his throne and great authority*" (Revelation 13:2).

Revelation provides the evidence to confirm that Satan is the one who has the secret power of lawlessness. Satan gives the Antichrist his power to deceive the world during the Great Tribulation.

Paul also ties the work of Satan and the Antichrist together, just as we have seen in Revelation. Paul says,

> *The coming of the lawless one* [Antichrist] *will be in accordance with the work of Satan displayed in all kinds of counterfeit miracles, signs and wonders, and in every sort of evil that deceives those who are perishing* (2 Thessalonians 2:9,10).

Therefore, we now know the identity of two of the three players in Paul's last days scenario:

1. He who is being held back   -   **Satan**
2. He who is doing the holding   -   ?
3. He who will be revealed   -   Antichrist

We should understand a little about Satan!

We know Satan has been at work from the time of Adam and Eve. Jesus said he has been at work from the beginning:

> *"You belong to your father, the devil, and you want to carry out your father's desire. He was a murderer* **from the beginning,** *not holding to the truth, for there is no truth in him"* (John 8:44).

Paul tells us that Satan is still at work today and that Satan is currently being held back or restrained.

> *For the secret power of lawlessness is* **already at work;** *but the one who* **now** *holds it back will continue to do so till he is taken out of the way* (2 Thessalonians 2:7).

There will come a three-and-a-half-year period in the future when Satan will no longer be held back. Therefore today, while we can clearly see that Satan is at work as he has been from the beginning, we should be aware that he is being held back or partially restrained. At the appointed time, Satan will no longer be held back. Then Satan will be unrestrained and the conditions on the earth will get dramatically worse. This will be the time of the Great Tribulation, when Satan and the Antichrist will try to destroy the people of God.

■ WHO IS HOLDING BACK SATAN?

So, now, the big question—who is holding back Satan, who has "*the secret power of lawlessness,*" until the appointed time?

In order to determine conclusively the identity of Satan's restrainer, we will examine various prophecies that describe what takes place at the time of the *abomination that causes desolation*. First, let's see what Paul says about this event.

Paul's version of the abomination

Paul describes the *abomination that causes desolation* as when the Antichrist is revealed.

> He will oppose and will exalt himself over everything that is called God or is worshiped, so that he sets himself up in God's temple, proclaiming himself to be God... And now you know what is holding him back, so that he may be revealed at the proper time. For the secret power of lawlessness is already at work; but the one who now holds it back will continue to do so till he is taken out of the way. And then the lawless one will be revealed (2 Thessalonians 2:4–8).

According to Paul, "*he*" who *now* holds Satan back will continue to do so until, the appointed time, when "*he*" no longer restrains Satan. When Satan is no longer restrained, the Antichrist will be revealed. Let's see how this looks on the timeline.

Last Days Timeline

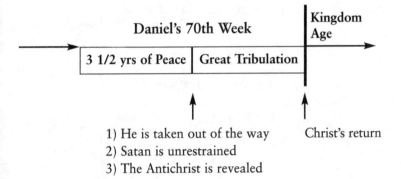

1) He is taken out of the way
2) Satan is unrestrained
3) The Antichrist is revealed

Since, Daniel wrote extensively about the rise to power of the Antichrist and was the first to prophesy about the *abomination that causes desolation*, let's examine his prophecies next.

Daniel's version of the abomination

In this key prophecy of Daniel, we see outlined the period called the Great Tribulation:

> *At that time Michael, the great prince who protects your people, will arise. There will be a time of distress* [tribulation] *such as has not happened from the beginning of nations until then. But at that time your people—everyone whose name is found written in the book—will be delivered. Multitudes who sleep in the dust of the earth will awake* (Daniel 12:1,2).

Daniel tells us that Michael, the protector of God's people, will arise to take his stand. Michael's call to action

comes at the time the Antichrist is revealed, before the Great
Tribulation. Since we already know that the Antichrist will
be revealed when Satan is unrestrained, we need to determine if something takes place between Michael and Satan at
that time. Let's look at the timeline again.

Last Days Timeline

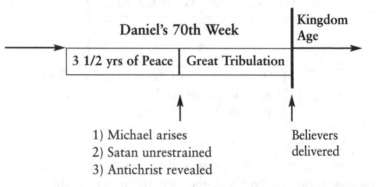

1) Michael arises
2) Satan unrestrained
3) Antichrist revealed

Believers
delivered

Because the Book of Revelation is the single most comprehensive description of the last days, we might expect to
find the answer to this mystery there.

John's version of the abomination

In chapter 12 of Revelation, John relates to us a vision
he saw in heaven to take place at the same time the *abomination that causes desolation* occurs on earth. Let's read
how he describes the scene:

> And there was war in heaven. Michael and his
> angels fought against the dragon, and the dragon
> and his angels fought back. But he [Satan] was not
> strong enough, and they lost their place in heaven.
> The great dragon was hurled down—that ancient

serpent called the devil, or Satan, who leads the whole world astray. He was hurled to the earth, and his angels with him (Revelation 12:7–9).

So, at the appointed time, Michael will arise and fight against Satan, and Satan will lose his place in heaven. Apparently, when Satan and his angels are hurled down to the earth, Michael will no longer be restraining Satan. Satan will then be able to go after the people of God without restraint.

When the dragon saw that he had been hurled to the earth, he pursued the woman [Israel] *who had given birth to the male child* [Jesus]. *The woman was given the two wings of a great eagle, so that she might fly to the place prepared for her in the desert, where she would be taken care of for a **time, times and half a time** [three and a half years], out of the serpent's reach…. Then the dragon was enraged at the woman* [Israel] *and went off to make war against the rest of her offspring* [the Church]—*those who obey God's commandments and hold to the testimony of Jesus* (Revelation 12:13–17).

When Michael throws Satan down to earth, Satan will become furious and pursue the destruction of Israel and the Church. We know this is the time of the Great Tribulation, because of what is happening and because John tells us how long this period of distress lasts. He says that this will be for *"a time, times and half a time,"* which is the same expression Daniel used when he wrote of the Great Tribulation period in Daniel 7:25 and 12:7. Therefore, we know that Michael will cast Satan down to earth at the same time of the *abomination that causes desolation*, when the Antichrist is revealed. In Revelation 13, John tells us even more about what happens during this last three and a half years of the Great Tribulation when Satan is unrestrained. Let's read it.

> *Men worshiped the dragon* [Satan] *because he had given authority to the beast* [Antichrist], *and they also worshiped the beast and asked, "Who is like the beast? Who can make war against him?" The beast was given a mouth to utter proud words and blasphemies and to exercise his authority for **forty-two months*** [three and a half years]. *He opened his mouth to blaspheme God, and to slander his name and his dwelling place and those who live in heaven. He was given power to make war against the saints and to conquer them. And he was given authority over every tribe, people, language and nation. All inhabitants of the earth will worship the beast—all whose names have not been written in the book of life belonging to the Lamb that was slain from the creation of the world. He, who has an ear, let him hear* (Revelation 13:4–9).

We have now seen the prophecies of Paul, Daniel and John regarding what happens at the time of the *abomination that causes desolation*. This is the sequence of events as they have been written:

1. Michael arises and throws Satan out of heaven to earth.
2. Satan gives his power to the Antichrist.
3. Antichrist is revealed at the *abomination that causes desolation*.
4. The Great Tribulation begins immediately and lasts three and a half years.
5. Christ returns on the Day of the Lord and gathers His elect.

Putting all this together, we have concluded that Michael is the one who is holding back Satan (the power of lawlessness) until the appointed time. Michael will then defeat Satan in battle and throw him and his angels down to earth. Satan's power of lawlessness will then be unrestrained and he will turn his fury on the people of God.

So now we know the mystery of all three players in Paul's last days scenario, as it is written.

1. He who is being held back   -   Satan
2. He who is doing the holding   -   **Michael**
3. He who will be revealed   -   Antichrist

Once again we see that the Bible is the best source for interpreting the Bible. The mystery regarding the identity of the one who restrains the secret power of lawlessness is clearly revealed.

During the Great Tribulation

As we return to 2 Thessalonians 2, we see that when the Antichrist is revealed, he will immediately begin the period known as the Great Tribulation. During this time, great deception and persecution will be perpetrated on the whole world by the Antichrist. Not only will there be great deception by the Antichrist, but God Himself will prevent those who have delighted in wickedness from knowing the truth.

The coming of the lawless one will be in accordance with the work of Satan displayed in all kinds of counterfeit miracles, signs and wonders, and in every sort of evil that deceives those who are perishing. They perish because they refused to love the truth and so be saved. For this reason God sends them a powerful delusion so that they will believe

*the lie and so that all will be condemned who have
not believed the truth but have delighted in wickedness* (2 Thessalonians 2:9–12).

As we compare this passage with the description in
Revelation, we see that there will be a considerable level of
supernatural activity during the Great Tribulation.

Because of the signs he [False Prophet] *was given
power to do on behalf of the first beast* [Antichrist],
*he deceived the inhabitants of the earth. He ordered
them to set up an image in honor of the beast that
was wounded by the sword and yet lived. He was
given power to give breath to the image of the first
beast, so that it could speak and cause all who
refused to worship the image to be killed*
(Revelation 13:14,15).

Because the consequences of not knowing the truth are
so terrible, Paul closes his letter with a very strong warning
and strict instructions to adhere to the Word of God:

*If anyone does not obey our instruction in this letter,
take special note of him. Do not associate with him,
in order that he may feel ashamed. Yet do not regard
him as an enemy, but warn him as a brother* (2
Thessalonians 2:14,15).

CHAPTER SEVEN

Just As He Announced to the Prophets

*But in the days when the seventh
angel is about to sound his trumpet,
the mystery of God will be accomplished,
just as he announced to his servants
the prophets* (Revelation 10:7).

So far we have studied Christ's teachings, Daniel's prophecies and Paul's writings regarding the last days. We know from our study that the next prophetic event predicted is the emergence of the fourth beast kingdom, which will come to dominate the whole world in the last days. Out of this kingdom, a leader known to Christians as the Antichrist will arise and persecute Israel and the followers of Christ during the Great Tribulation.

We will now examine what the Lord has *"announced to His servants the prophets"* about the last days. Because we have already studied Daniel's prophecies, we will emphasize the other Old Testament prophets, particularly Isaiah.

Before we begin this part of our study, let's review the key elements of the last days. Jesus taught that there would be two ages on the earth—the present age, in which we now live, and the coming age of righteousness. Jesus often referred to the coming age in terms like the "Kingdom of God" or the "Kingdom of Heaven."

However, just before the coming age of righteousness, there will be a seven-year period we call Daniel's seventieth week. The last three and a half years of Daniel's seventieth week is the Great Tribulation. After the Great Tribulation, Jesus will return to establish the Kingdom of God on earth. Let's look at the timeline below.

Last Days Timeline

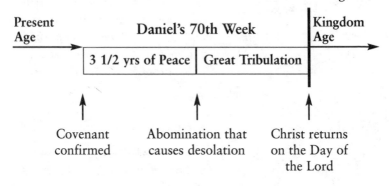

We are currently in the Present Age, just before Daniel's seventieth week. We know that prior to Daniel's seventieth week, the fourth beast kingdom will come into being (Daniel 7:23–25). Out of this fourth beast kingdom, the Antichrist will rise to power. Once in power, he will confirm a covenant of peace with Israel. Then in the middle of the last seven years, the Antichrist will set himself up as God in the temple in Jerusalem. This event is referred to as the *abomination that causes desolation* as spoken of by the prophet Daniel (Daniel 9:27). The Antichrist will then reign supreme on earth until Christ returns on the Day of the Lord.

As we study the writings of the Old Testament prophets, we need to recognize they wrote from the perspective of the nation of Israel. During the times of the prophets, Israel was engaged in life-and-death struggles with its neighbors. The prophets often intertwined predictions of Israel's near-term future with predictions of the last days. Therefore, as we study their prophecies, we must look for details that match what we already know about the last days. By comparing these prophecies with what we know from other prophecies, we will be able to determine if the prophecy is about the last days or not.

There is something else we need to keep in mind as we continue our study—while each prophet had different perspectives, each wrote about the same last days; there is only one last days scenario from God as revealed in His Word. Since all describe the same thing, we can expect to see similarities in what they describe. Also, remember that no prophecy of God came by man's own understanding (2 Peter 1:21), indicating that all biblical last days prophecy has its origin in the Holy Spirit.

When it comes to prophecies depicting the two comings of our Lord, Isaiah wrote abundantly of both Advents. Isaiah's prophecies are so descriptive of the First Advent that the Lord's suffering and crucifixion appear to be written as historical narrative. So extensive are his writings that people even call the Book of Isaiah the "Gospel of the Old Testament." For the purposes of our study, we are very grateful that Isaiah was even more prolific in his writings of the last days and Christ's Second Advent. For that reason, we will give priority to his writings in this portion of our study.

On May 14, 1948, after almost 1,900 years of exile, Israel once again became a nation established in the Promised Land. From that moment, the Jewish nation entered into a series of continuing life-and-death struggles with its Arab neighbors. Israel's current struggles seem forebodingly similar to what we find prophesied regarding the last days. We will see from the prophets that Israel's struggles will continue until she obtains a temporary peace by signing a covenant with the Antichrist.

■ THE COVENANT IS CONFIRMED

Let's read how Isaiah describes Israel's relationship with the Antichrist. Isaiah refers to this future world leader as "*the Assyrian.*"

> *Woe to the Assyrian* [Antichrist]... *I send him against a godless nation, I dispatch him against a people who anger me, to seize loot and snatch plunder, and to trample them down like mud in the streets. ...Therefore, the Lord, the* LORD *Almighty, will send a wasting disease upon his sturdy warriors; under his pomp a fire will be kindled like a blazing flame. ...In that day the remnant of Israel, the survivors of the house of Jacob,* **will no longer rely on him** [Antichrist] *who struck them down but will truly rely on the* LORD, *the Holy One of Israel* (Isaiah 10:5–20).

Isaiah is telling us that the people of Israel will at first rely on the Antichrist for their security. This is likely a reference to the covenant of peace that the Antichrist will confirm at the beginning of the last seven years; see Daniel 9:27. As we know from Daniel's prophecy, this peace will last only three and a half years, and then the Antichrist will turn against Israel. When the Antichrist turns against Israel, there will be a period of unprecedented distress and persecution we call the Great Tribulation (Matthew 24:21 and Daniel 12:1).

Another of Isaiah's prophecies captures the very nature of this covenant with the Antichrist when we are told that the leaders of Israel will boast about the covenant they have made:

Therefore, hear the word of the LORD, *you scoffers who rule this people in Jerusalem. You boast, We have entered into **a covenant with death**, with the grave we have made an agreement. ...**Your covenant with death** will be annulled; your agreement with the grave will not stand...* (Isaiah 28:14–18).

Isaiah says this treaty would be "*a covenant with death*" because, as we will see, death will be its outcome. When the Antichrist comes against Israel, it will be the worst slaughter of the people of God in human history. Isaiah 10 and 28 tell us that the covenant with death—Israel's reliance on the Antichrist—will not last. The peace under the Antichrist will be cut short, the Antichrist will punish Israel during the Great Tribulation and then God will punish the Antichrist. When God comes against the Antichrist, God will "*on that day*" be Israel's protector. Then the remnant of Israel will recognize the Lord as their Messiah and call on Him as Jesus predicted (Matthew 23:39).

This same scenario, which Isaiah describes in chapter 10 between Israel and the Antichrist, is also found in Ezekiel 38 and 39:

*Son of man, set your face against Gog [Antichrist], of the land of Magog, You will say, "I will invade a land of unwalled villages; I will attack a peaceful and unsuspecting people—all of them living without walls and without gates and bars. I will **plunder and loot**... In that day, when my people Israel are living* *in safety, will you not take notice of it? You will come from your place in the far north, you and many nations with you, all of them riding on horses, a great horde, a mighty army. In my zeal and fiery wrath I declare that at that time there shall be a great earthquake in the land of Israel. I will execute judgment upon him with plague and bloodshed; I will pour down torrents of rain, hailstones and burning sulfur on him and on his troops and on the many nations with him. And so I will show my greatness and my holiness, and I will make myself known in the sight of many nations. Then they will know that I am the* LORD (Ezekiel 38:2–23).

Ezekiel tells us that God will cause Gog—the leader of the land of Magog—to attack Israel, to *"plunder and loot"* just as Isaiah, also, described. Isaiah said God will cause the Assyrian to *"plunder and loot"* (compare Isaiah 10:6 and Ezekiel 38:12). Ezekiel tells us that God will cause Gog to come against Israel when she is at peace and living safely. In Isaiah 10:20, the implication is also that Israel will be relying on the Antichrist for her peace and safety until he comes against her. However, God will not allow Israel's complete destruction and He will send a wasting *"disease or plague"* against the Antichrist and his warriors (compare Isaiah 10:16 and Ezekiel 38:22). First, the Antichrist will ensure Israel's peace—then attempt to destroy her. After the Great Tribulation, God will fight for Israel and she will know that Jesus is Lord. Compare these passages and see the similarities.

During Isaiah's time, he referred to the Assyrians and their leader *"the Assyrian"* in relation to the last days. During Ezekiel's time, he referred to the land of Magog and their leader "*Gog*" in relation to the last days. When Isaiah refers to Assyria and Ezekiel refers to the land of Magog, they both refer to the same people and territory, which is located just southwest of the Caspian Sea. Today, Iran occupies this territory.

Now, about the time of peace and security between the covenant and the *abomination that causes desolation*, the Scripture tells us very little. We can, however, determine that by the time of the *abomination that causes desolation*, the Jewish people will be practicing temple worship in the temple in Jerusalem. Therefore, even though we don't know when temple worship will begin, we do know that it will be practiced during at least some of the time covered by the covenant.

It is very interesting to recall that the temple mount was one of the topics of negotiation just before the Israeli and Palestinian peace talks broke down in January 2001. Based on what is written in Scripture, we can expect that the topic of the temple mount will be discussed again in the future.

The last of Isaiah's prophecies describes events that will be fulfilled during the last days. As chapter 66 opens, Isaiah describes God's perspective of Jewish temple worship and animal sacrifice during the last days:

> *This is what the* LORD *says: "Heaven is my throne, and the earth is my footstool. Where is the house you will build for me? Where will my resting place be? Has not my hand made all these things, and so they came into being?" declares the* LORD*. "This is the one I esteem: he who is humble and contrite in spirit, and trembles at my word. But whoever sacrifices a bull is like one who kills a man, and whoever offers a lamb, like one who breaks a dog's neck; whoever makes a grain offering is like one who pre-*

sents pig's blood, and whoever burns memorial incense, like one who worships an idol. They have chosen their own ways, and their souls delight in their abominations (Isaiah 66:1–3).

The Lord is severely rebuking Israel for rebuilding the temple and reinstating temple worship. God is angry with Israel and He will soon punish her by bringing the Antichrist against her in what is also called the "time of Jacob's trouble."

■ THE ABOMINATION THAT CAUSES DESOLATION

Before the *abomination that causes desolation*, the Jewish nation will be at peace, secure in their land. Then the Antichrist and his army will come and surround Jerusalem. He will enter the city and go to the temple mount. Now, let's read how Isaiah describes what occurs in Jerusalem and from the temple when the Antichrist sets himself up in the temple of God, declaring himself to be God.

"Hear that uproar from the city, hear that noise from the temple! It is the sound of the LORD repaying his enemies all they deserve" (Isaiah 66:6). The persecution and death of the Great Tribulation immediately follows the *abomination that causes desolation*. This is when God will repay Israel's unbelief by using the Antichrist to punish them. Jeremiah also describes the same thing when he tells us that the time of peace will turn to fear during the *time of Jacob's trouble*. Jeremiah, like Isaiah and Ezekiel, also indicates that Israel will not be totally destroyed, because the Lord will deliver a remnant out of the Great Tribulation.

This is what the LORD says: Cries of fear are heard—terror, not peace. ...How awful that day will be! None will be like it. It will be a time of trouble for Jacob, but he will be saved out of it (Jeremiah 30:5,7).

From Daniel's prophecies, we know the Great Tribulation will be a time of unequalled distress lasting three and a half years. Jesus also indicates that the Great Tribulation will be so horrific that if it were not cut short, no one would survive. Let's take another look at the timeline to see where we are as we prepare to study what will take place after the Great Tribulation.

Last Days Timeline

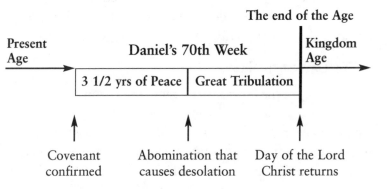

■ SIGNS BEFORE THE DAY OF THE LORD

Before we begin to study the Day of the Lord, we should note that the Old Testament prophets specifically tell us about two signs which will come before "the great and dreadful Day of the Lord." Malachi prophesies, *"See, I will send you the prophet Elijah **before** that great and dreadful day of the LORD comes"* (Malachi 4:5).

The prophet Joel prophesies that the sun, moon and stars will be darkened before the great and dreadful Day of the Lord. When we read prophecies regarding the Day of the Lord, we frequently see the sign of the darkening of the sun, moon and stars. However, Joel is the first to tell us that this sign will come **before** *"the great and dreadful day of the Lord."*

> *I will show wonders in the heavens and the earth, blood and fire and billows of smoke. The sun will be turned to darkness and the moon to blood **before** the coming of the great and dreadful day of the* LORD (Joel 2:30,31).

In our study of the prophets, we have now come through the Great Tribulation and are poised at the very end of the age, as we wait for the Day of the Lord to break out over the whole world.

■ THE DAY OF THE LORD

The Day of the Lord is an extremely important part of the biblical record and God's plan. Without a good basic understanding of *"the Day of the Lord,"* no one can properly understand the gospel of Jesus Christ. Yet, many people in the household of God have not even heard about the *"Day of the Lord"* and its significance to the gospel of Jesus Christ.

The Day of the Lord is the prophetic event referred to in Scripture so many times by the prophets that they often abbreviated it by writing, *"that day"* or *"the day."* In the New Testament, the Day of the Lord is also referred to as *"the day of the Lord Jesus Christ," "the day of the Lord Jesus," "the day of Christ Jesus," "the day of Christ,"* and *"the day of God."* **There is only one Day of the Lord!**

As the world goes through the Great Tribulation and approaches the Day of the Lord, conditions on the earth will become catastrophic. God will allow great destruction through the Antichrist during this time of severe trial and testing which will come upon the whole world (Revelation 3:10).

As we examine the writings of the Old Testament prophets about the coming of the Day of the Lord, we need to be alert to what is written. If we are not careful, we may become confused about exactly what is being described.

There are several reasons to study these writings carefully:

1. The general world conditions during the Great Tribulation will become so catastrophic that we could confuse them with God's wrath.
2. Biblical prophecy often moves back and forward in time as God describes events which will take place. What is written rarely follows a strict chronological order. Therefore we need to read prophecy in the context of the whole Word of God.
3. There are so many events taking place before and during the Day of the Lord that the amount of activity can be overwhelming.

Let's review what we already know as we prepare to study the coming Day of the Lord. The darkening of the sun, moon and stars will be a sign that the Day of the Lord is imminent. We also know that before Jesus returns, He will leave heaven accompanied by His angels and appear in the clouds of the sky. While He is still in the sky, He will send His angels to gather all believers to Himself. With these things in mind, let's examine what the prophets say about the Day of the Lord and Christ's return.

The Day of the Lord—He comes down from heaven

David tells us that the Lord will come down out of heaven and touch the earth when it is time for Him to rout His enemies:

Part your heavens, O LORD, and come down; touch the mountains, so that they smoke. Send forth lightning and scatter the enemies; shoot your arrows and rout them. Reach down your hand from on high; deliver me and rescue me from the mighty waters, from the hands of foreigners (Psalm 144:5–7).

From these prophecies, we see that the Lord will come down from heaven to earth when He returns. David, in Psalm 144, and Isaiah both seem to be indicating that the resurrection of believers will also occur at this time. *"Look! The LORD is coming from his dwelling place; he comes down and treads the high places of the earth"* (Micah 1:3); *"But your dead will live; their bodies will rise... See, the LORD is coming out of his dwelling to punish the people of the earth for their sins"* (Isaiah 26:19,21).

The LORD will roar from on high; he will thunder from his holy dwelling... he will bring judgment on all mankind and put the wicked to the sword, declares the LORD. This is what the LORD Almighty says: 'Look!' Disaster is spreading from nation to nation; a mighty storm is rising from the ends of the earth (Jeremiah 25:30–32).

David also prophesied that the Lord would remain at the Father's right hand in heaven until it is time for Him to put His enemies under His feet (Psalm 110). This sounds similar to Peter, in Acts 3:21, when he tells us that the Lord must remain in heaven until it is time to restore everything. Both of these passages place the Coming of Christ following the Great Tribulation when He destroys His enemies and restores everything to Israel. Compare the timing of these two verses:

The LORD says to my Lord: 'Sit at my right hand until I make your enemies a footstool for your feet' ... The Lord is at your right hand; he will crush kings on the day of his wrath. He will judge the nations, heaping up the dead and crushing the rulers (Psalm 110:1,5).

He must remain in heaven until the time comes for God to restore everything, as he promised long ago through his holy prophets (Acts 3:21).

The Day of the Lord—the trumpet call

We have seen that, when Jesus appears to gather all believers, a trumpet call will signal the gathering and the resurrection. Of course, we already know from the New Testament that it is the last trumpet which signals the gathering. So, let's read how the prophets describe the sounding of the trumpet call, which signals the gathering of believers to Christ.

*All you people of the world, you who live on the earth, when a banner is raised on the mountains, you will see it, and when a **trumpet** sounds, you will hear it...* (Isaiah 18:3).

*In that day the LORD will thresh from the flowing Euphrates to the Wadi of Egypt, and you, O Israelites, will be gathered up one by one. And in that day a **great trumpet** will sound* (Isaiah 27:12,13).

*Then the LORD will appear over them; his arrow will flash like lightning. The Sovereign LORD will sound **the trumpet**; ... The LORD their God will save them on that day as the flock of his people* (Zechariah 9:14,16).

Before them the earth shakes, the sky trembles, the
sun and moon are darkened, and the stars no longer
shine. The LORD *thunders at the head of his army;*
his forces are beyond number, and mighty are those
who obey his command. The day of the LORD *is*
great; it is dreadful. Who can endure it? Blow **the**
trumpet *in Zion, declare a holy fast, and call a*
sacred assembly. Gather the people, consecrate the
assembly; bring together the elders (Joel 2:10–16).

When we connect these prophecies, we get a good picture of what we have already received from Jesus and the
apostle Paul.

The Day of the Lord—the resurrection gathering

When the Lord comes down out of heaven, the trumpet
will sound and all believers will be gathered to Him in their
resurrection bodies. We see the first mention of this resurrection change in the Book of Job, when he describes the
resurrection of the dead. In the Old Testament we find
numerous descriptions of the resurrection of the dead. Let's
read how the prophets describe the raising of the dead.

Job tells us that the resurrection of believers will be at
the end of the age, when Christ comes to earth. Job also tells
us that after God's anger (with Israel) has passed, there will
be a renewal. Job also indicates this renewal will include his
resurrected body:

If only you would hide me in the grave and conceal me
till your anger has passed! All the days of my hard ser-
vice I will wait for my renewal to come (Job 14:13,14).

I know that my Redeemer lives, and that in the end
he will stand upon the earth. And after my skin has

been destroyed, yet in my flesh I will see God; I myself will see him with my own eyes (Job 19:25–27).

In the Psalms we are told that the Lord will come in the clouds in the brightness of His glory as He thunders down from heaven. When He comes, He is described as reaching down to take hold of the believers as they are gathered to Himself in the resurrection.

Out of the brightness of his presence clouds advanced, with hailstones and bolts of lightning. The LORD thundered from heaven; the voice of the Most High resounded... He reached down from on high and took hold of me; he drew me out of deep waters (Psalms 18:12,13,16).

And I, in righteousness I will see your face; when I awake, I will be satisfied with seeing your likeness (Psalm 17:15).

But God will redeem my life from the grave; he will surely take me to himself (Psalm 49:15).

Isaiah, who always provides vivid descriptions, tells us of the coming of Christ. See how he develops this picture of the Lord coming out of heaven to raise the believers in the resurrection and to punish the sinners:

But your dead will live; their bodies will rise. You, who dwell in the dust, wake up and shout for joy. Your dew is like the dew of the morning; the earth will give birth to her dead. Go, my people, enter your rooms and shut the doors behind you; hide yourselves for a little while until his wrath has passed by. See, the LORD is coming out of his dwelling to punish the people of the earth for their sins. The earth will dis-

close the bloodshed upon her; she will conceal her slain no longer (Isaiah 26:19–21).

The idea of the *"resurrection of the dead"* is well developed in the Old Testament. When Daniel describes the resurrection, below, he places it as occurring after the time of unprecedented distress:

Therefore prophesy and say to them: This is what the Sovereign LORD says: O my people, I am going to open your graves and bring you up from them (Ezekiel 37:12).

At that time Michael, the great prince who protects your people, will arise. There will be a time of distress [tribulation] *such as has not happened from the beginning of nations until then. But at that time your people—everyone whose name is found written in the book—will be delivered. Multitudes who sleep in the dust of the earth will awake: some to everlasting life, others to shame and everlasting contempt* (Daniel 12:1,2).

I will ransom them from the power of the grave; I will redeem them from death. Where, O death, are your plagues? Where, O grave, is your destruction? (Hosea 13:14).

The resurrection of the living believers is not fully explained in Scripture until the New Testament. However, there are some indications from the prophets that the believers alive at that time of the resurrection would also be included. *"What man can live and not see death, or save himself from the power of the grave?"* (Psalm 89:48).

I will not die but live, and will proclaim what the

LORD *has done. The* LORD *has chastened me severely, but he has not given me over to death* (Psalm 118:17,18).

Psalm 144 not only describes the Lord coming down from heaven to earth, but also indicates that the Lord will rescue the believer from foreigners. This sounds very much like what the Lord will do when He gathers the living believers from the earth and out of the Great Tribulation.

Part your heavens, O LORD, *and come down; touch the mountains, so that they smoke. Send forth lightning and scatter the enemies; shoot your arrows and rout them. Reach down your hand from on high; deliver me and rescue me from the mighty waters, from the hands of foreigners* (Psalm 144:5–7).

Another prophecy in the Psalms pulls together the coming of the Lord and the resurrection of the living and the dead. When we compare this psalm to Jesus' same description in the Olivet Discourse, we find confirmation that the resurrection includes all believers, living and dead. Let's compare the two passages to see how the living are gathered from the earth and the dead are gathered from heaven at Christ's return.

From Zion, perfect in beauty, God shines forth. Our God comes and will not be silent; a fire devours before him, and around him a tempest rages. He summons the heavens above [dead in Christ], *and the earth* [living in Christ], *that he may judge his people: Gather to me my consecrated ones, who made a covenant with me by sacrifice* (Psalm 50:2–5).

They will see the Son of Man coming on the clouds of

the sky, with power and great glory. And he will send his angels with a loud trumpet call, and they will gather his elect from the four winds [living in Christ], *from one end of the heavens* [dead in Christ] *to the other* (Matthew 24:30,31).

If we lay the key elements of these two passages side by side, we can see clearly that they both describe the coming of our Lord and the gathering of all believers from the earth and from heaven.

Psalm 50	Matthew 24
Our God comes	Son of Man coming
God shines forth	They will see the Son of Man
Will not be silent	With a loud trumpet call
Gather His people	Gather His elect
From the earth	From the four winds of earth
The heavens above	The heavens

So, with just a little help from the New Testament, we are able to see the resurrection of the dead and the Rapture of the living at Christ's appearing, even in the Old Testament.

After the angels have gathered the believers to the Lord in the air, the Lord will continue to earth with His holy ones. Let's see how Zechariah describes this.

On that day his feet will stand on the Mount of Olives, east of Jerusalem, and the Mount of Olives will be split in two from east to west, ...Then the LORD *my God will come, and all the holy ones with him* (Zechariah 14:4,5).

Zechariah reveals in this passage that Jesus will return to earth in the same way that He left as described in Acts

1:11. Not only will He return in the same way He left but He will return to the same place—the Mount of Olives. Ezekiel tells us from there the Lord will enter the temple through the eastern gate.

> *Then the man brought me to the gate facing east, and I saw the glory of the God of Israel coming from the east. His voice was like the roar of rushing waters, and the land was radiant with his glory... The glory of the LORD entered the temple through the gate facing east. Then the Spirit lifted me up and brought me into the inner court, and the glory of the LORD filled the temple. While the man was standing beside me, I heard someone speaking to me from inside the temple. He said: "Son of man, this is the place of my throne and the place for the soles of my feet. This is where I will live among the Israelites forever"* (Ezekiel 43:1–7).

From these passages we can establish that after we are gathered to the Lord in the air, we will continue with Him when He descends to the Mount of Olives and enters Mount Zion through the eastern gate. When we connect these last days prophecies, we get a magnificent picture of the Lord's triumphant return. However, there is still more.

The Day of the Lord—The wedding feast

Now that all believers have been gathered to Christ and we have accompanied Him to Mount Zion, let's look at what happens next.

> *On this mountain* [Zion], *the LORD Almighty will prepare a feast of rich food for all peoples, a banquet of aged wine—the best of meats and the finest*

of wines. On this mountain he will destroy the
shroud that enfolds all peoples, the sheet that
covers all nations; he will swallow up death forever
(Isaiah 25:6–8).

Isaiah describes a lavish feast that the Lord prepares, which can only be the wedding feast of Jesus Christ and His bride, the Church. Jesus taught us about this wedding banquet several times; see Matthew 8:11 and 25:10. The wedding banquet is also referred to in Revelation 19:9. While some have mistakenly imagined that the wedding feast takes place in heaven, it is clear from Scripture that it takes place on Mount Zion in Jerusalem.

As Isaiah tells us about the wedding feast, he also describes the resurrection changes that will take place in the believers. First, he says that the shroud, or sheet, that covers the people will be destroyed—indicating that the shroud will be removed. This conveys the same idea Paul expressed regarding the change we will experience: *"Now I know in part; then I shall know fully"* (1 Corinthians 13:12). What was previously shrouded from our view will be revealed. Another aspect of the resurrection change is that believers will no longer be subject to death—*"he will swallow up death forever"* (Isaiah 25:8). Therefore, just as we saw in 1 Corinthians 15:54, at the time of resurrection the believers will no longer be subject to death and they *"shall know fully."* Isaiah also places the change in the believers on the Day of the Lord; in 25:9 he says this will happen in *"that day."* Isaiah makes other references to aspects of the Day of the Lord and the coming Kingdom when he says, *"the LORD will wipe away the tears, and remove disgrace from the earth."*

The Day of the Lord—is one Day

Before we go any further with our study regarding the Day of the Lord, we should look closely at what the prophets say regarding its duration. Is the Day of the Lord a protracted period, or is it a twenty-four hour day? While a great deal will happen on the Day of the Lord, we can rest assured that the Lord will not need a consultant to accomplish His plan on time. In describing the events of the Day of the Lord, Isaiah says that it will happen "*in a single day.*"

> *The Light of Israel will become a fire, their Holy One a flame;* **in a single day** *it will burn and consume his thorns and his briers. The splendor of his forests and fertile fields it will completely destroy, as when a sick man wastes away. And the remaining trees of his forests will be so few that a child could write them down. In that day the remnant of Israel, the survivors of the house of Jacob, will no longer rely on him who struck them down but will truly rely on the* LORD, *the Holy One of Israel* (Isaiah 10:17–20).

Zechariah also tells us that "*on that day,*" when Christ comes down from heaven and establishes the Kingdom on earth, "*It will be a unique day,*" which definitely qualifies him as the prophet of understatement.

> **On that day** *his feet will stand on the Mount of Olives, east of Jerusalem, and the Mount of Olives will be split in two from east to west ...Then the* LORD *my God will come, and all the holy ones with him.... On that day there will be no light, no cold or frost.* **It will be a unique day,** *without daytime or nighttime—a day known to the* LORD. *When*

*evening comes, there will be light... The LORD will
be king over the whole earth. On that day there will
be one LORD, and his name the only name*
(Zechariah 14:4–9).

Zechariah wrote extensively concerning the Day of the
Lord and in this passage, he says the Lord alone will be
King over the whole earth on that day. Therefore, those
who say the Day of the Lord includes the Great Tribulation
should consider this passage, because, how will it be possible for the Antichrist to rule the whole world at the same
time Christ is King of the whole earth?

The Day of the Lord—the Wrath of God

As we read through the writings of the prophets, we
also find that the Day of the Lord is the time of God's
wrath. The wrath that comes with the Day of the Lord will
not be destruction by water, as in the days of Noah, but by
fire (2 Peter 3:6,7). This destruction and judgment will
consume everything that is not of Christ. The final aspect
of God's judgment on the nations will be the battle of
Armageddon.

Once again we find that Isaiah provides a thorough
description of the Day of the Lord. So comprehensive is his
description that it requires no commentary. As we read
these passages, we will see vivid descriptions of the wrath of
God as well as other aspects of that day which we have
already covered. Read this sample of Isaiah's description of
the coming Day of the Lord:

*Go into the rocks, hide in the ground from dread of
the LORD and the splendor of his majesty! The
LORD Almighty has a day in store for all the proud
and lofty, for all that is exalted (and they will be*

*humbled), ... The arrogance of man will be brought
low and the pride of men humbled; the LORD alone
will be exalted in that day, Men will flee to caves in
the rocks and to holes in the ground from dread of
the LORD* (Isaiah 2:10–19).

*I have commanded my holy ones; I have summoned
my warriors to carry out my wrath—those who
rejoice in my triumph. Listen, an uproar among the
kingdoms, like nations massing together! The LORD
Almighty is mustering an army for war. ...Wail, for
the day of the LORD is near; it will come like
destruction from the Almighty... See, the day of the
LORD is coming—a cruel day, with wrath and fierce
anger—to make the land desolate and destroy the
sinners within it. The stars of heaven and their con-
stellations will not show their light. The rising sun
will be darkened and the moon will not give its
light. I will punish the world for its evil, the wicked
for their sins... Therefore I will make the heavens
tremble; and the earth will shake from its place at
the wrath of the LORD Almighty, in the day of his
burning anger* (Isaiah 13:3–13).

*They will all be left to the mountain birds of prey and
to the wild animals; the birds will feed on them all
summer, the wild animals all winter* (Isaiah 18:6).

*In that day the LORD will punish the powers in the
heavens above and the kings on the earth below.
They will be herded together like prisoners bound in
a dungeon; they will be shut up in prison and be
punished after many days. The moon will be
abashed, the sun ashamed; for the LORD Almighty*

*will reign on Mount Zion and in Jerusalem, and
before its elders, gloriously* (Isaiah 24:21–23).

So far we have learned from the prophets that on the
Day of the Lord: (1) The Lord will appear in the sky and
gather all believers to Himself. (2) Then, accompanied by
the saints, He will return to earth, prepare the wedding feast
and establish the Kingdom of God on the earth. (3) He will
also punish the unbelieving and disobedient world. As the
prophets say, this day will be both great and terrible. Great,
for it is the day of deliverance for the people of God, and
dreadful, for it is the day of God's wrath for the unbelievers.
Of course, Isaiah captures the idea when he calls it "*the day
of reckoning*"—redemption for the righteous and punishment for the unrighteous. Several of the prophets have captured these two aspects of the Day of the Lord. Starting
with Isaiah, let's see how they describe the Day of the Lord.

*See, the Sovereign LORD comes with power, and his
arm rules for him. See, his reward is with him, and
his recompense accompanies him* (Isaiah 40:10).

*Why are your garments red, like those of one
treading the winepress? ... For the day of vengeance
was in my heart, and the year of my redemption has
come* (Isaiah 63:2,4).

*I will show wonders in the heavens and the earth,
blood and fire and billows of smoke. The sun will be
turned to darkness and the moon to blood before
the coming of the great and dreadful day of the
LORD* (Joel 2:30,31).

*On that day I will set out to destroy all the nations
that attack Jerusalem. And I will pour out on the*

house of David and the inhabitants of Jerusalem a
spirit of grace and supplication. They will look on
me, the one they have pierced, (Zechariah 12:9, 10).

The Day of the Lord—Kingdom of God

The long-awaited and much-desired aspect of the Day
of the Lord is the coming Kingdom of God on earth. Isaiah
tells us that in the last days, the Kingdom of the Lord will
be established, emanating from Jerusalem and encom-
passing all the nations of the world. Isaiah says, "*the LORD*
Almighty will reign on Mount Zion and in Jerusalem, and
before its elders, gloriously" (Isaiah 24:23).

In the last days the mountain of the Lord's temple
will be established as chief among the mountains; ...
it will be raised above the hills, and all nations will
stream to it. He will judge between the nations and
will settle disputes for many peoples... Nation will
not take up sword against nation, nor will they train
for war anymore (Isaiah 2:2–4).

The word "*mountain*" in this context, like many places in
Scripture, is synonymous with "*kingdom*" and, therefore, the
"*mountain of the Lord*" also means the "*Kingdom of God*"
(Isaiah 13:4).

On that day, Christ will establish on earth the long-
awaited Kingdom of God. Isaiah vividly describes the characteristics of this earthly Kingdom as he heralds its arrival.
The vision of the Kingdom is that of a Kingdom of righteousness, where the curse of sin will be lifted and everything will be restored. The restoration of everything seems
to signify that God will be restoring the earth to its original
state, as it was in the Garden of Eden before man first dis-

obeyed God. The restoration of everything also means that Christ will rule the world from the throne of David in Jerusalem. From these passages below, we receive a preview of some of the Kingdom characteristics we can expect:

The wolf will live with the lamb, the leopard will lie down with the goat, the calf and the lion and the yearling together; and a little child will lead them. The cow will feed with the bear, their young will lie down together, and the lion will eat straw like the ox. The infant will play near the hole of the cobra, and the young child put his hand into the viper's nest. They will neither harm nor destroy on all my holy mountain, for the earth will be full of the knowledge of the LORD as the waters cover the sea. In that day the Root of Jesse will stand as a banner for the peoples; the nations will rally to him, and his place of rest will be glorious (Isaiah 11:6–10).

Never again will there be in it an infant who lives but a few days, or an old man who does not live out his years; he who dies at a hundred will be thought a mere youth; he who fails to reach a hundred will be considered accursed. They will build houses and dwell in them; they will plant vineyards and eat their fruit. No longer will they build houses and others live in them, or plant and others eat. For as the days of a tree, so will be the days of my people; my chosen ones will long enjoy the works of their hands. They will not toil in vain or bear children doomed to misfortune; for they will be a people blessed by the LORD, they and their descendants with them. Before they call I will answer; while they are still speaking I will hear. The wolf and the lamb will feed together, and the lion will eat straw like the ox, but dust will be the serpent's food. They will neither harm nor destroy on all my holy mountain, says the LORD (Isaiah 65:20–25).

The Kingdom of God as described in Scripture is a Kingdom of righteousness in a revitalized earth—a world difficult for us to imagine as we look on the present world around us. Nevertheless, it is easy to see that the Kingdom will be infinitely better than our current reality. One passage that comes to mind while reflecting on the Kingdom is in 1 Corinthians 2:

None of the rulers of this age understood it, for if they had, they would not have crucified the Lord of glory. However, as it is written: "No eye has seen, no ear has heard, no mind has conceived what God has prepared for those who love him" (1 Corinthians 2:8,9).

In this brief study of the prophets, we have seen that their writings provide clear and detailed descriptions of the last days and the return of Christ. When we connect their descriptions with the rest of Scripture, we find an amazingly comprehensive picture of the time leading up to the return of Christ.

■ WATCH OUT THAT NO ONE DECEIVES YOU

Before we conclude this portion of our study of the last days, there is another very important message that the prophets received from God. They not only warned the people about what was coming, but they also warned the people and their leaders of their need to repent and turn back to God. God's message to His people of that day is the same message He has for us today. The apparent similarities between the Jewish church of their day and the Christian church of today should convict us to repent and turn back to God. As we consider these similarities we should ask, what if the Christian church today is as hard-hearted and stiff-necked as the Jewish church was in their day? Let's pray that this aspect of history will not repeat itself.

Now let's read from the prophets to see what else God is saying to us about the last days. At least two reasons indicate that these messages are also for today. First, the spiritual conditions are the same today as they were then. Second, these prophecies connect themselves to the events that relate to the Day of the Lord and the last days. First, let's read what Jeremiah has written about the false prophets.

> This is what the LORD Almighty says: "Do not listen to what the prophets are prophesying to you; they fill you with false hopes. They speak visions from their own minds, not from the mouth of the LORD. They keep saying to those who despise me, 'The LORD says: You will have peace.' And to all who follow the stubbornness of their hearts they say, 'No harm will come to you.' But which of them has stood in the council of the LORD to see or to hear his word? Who has listened and heard his word? See, the storm of the LORD will burst out in wrath, a whirlwind swirling down on the heads of the wicked. The anger of the LORD will not turn back until he fully accomplishes the purposes of his heart. In days to come you will understand it clearly. I did not send these prophets, yet they have run with their message; I did not speak to them, yet they have prophesied. ..." I have heard what the prophets say who prophesy lies in my name.

They say, 'I had a dream! I had a dream!' How
long will this continue in the hearts of these lying
prophets, who prophesy the delusions of their own
minds?" ..."Therefore," declares the LORD, *"I am*
against the prophets who steal from one another
words supposedly from me. Yes," declares the
LORD, *"I am against the prophets who wag their*
own tongues and yet declare, 'The LORD *declares'"*
(Jeremiah 23:16–31).

This passage from Jeremiah reveals several characteristics of false prophets. Let's list the characteristics to get a clear understanding.

The false prophets:

- Claimed to have heard the Word of God, but had not.
- Attribute words to God He had not spoken.
- Prophesy out of their imagination.
- Say "The LORD says: You will have peace," and "No harm will come to you."
- Take from one another words supposedly from God.
- Have God against them and His wrath will be on their heads.

Now consider these characteristics, in light of what we observe today. **Ask yourself these questions:**

- Who is proclaiming what is going to happen in the name of the Lord?
- Who is proclaiming the Word just as it is written in Scripture?
- Who is saying that we will be gone before the tribulation comes?

• Who takes words from another supposedly from God?

In answering these questions, I have some very good news! Today, since we have the complete written Scripture, we are all able to determine who the false prophet is and who is not. Therefore, when someone says, "The Bible says…" when it does not, this is prophesying falsely.

In Ezekiel's time there were also people who falsely proclaimed the Word of God. Let's read from Ezekiel what God had to say about the foolish prophets.

> *"Son of man, prophesy against the prophets of Israel who are now prophesying. Say to those who prophesy out of their own imagination: 'Hear the word of the* LORD! *This is what the Sovereign* LORD *says: Woe to the foolish prophets who follow their own spirit and have seen nothing! Your prophets, O Israel, are like jackals among ruins. …Their visions are false and their divinations a lie. They say, "The* LORD *declares," when the* LORD *has not sent them; yet they expect their words to be fulfilled. Have you not seen false visions and uttered lying divinations when you say, "The* **LORD** *declares," though I have not spoken?* "'Therefore this is what the Sovereign* LORD *says: Because of your false words and lying visions, I am against you, declares the Sovereign* LORD. *My hand will be against the prophets who see false visions and utter lying divinations. They will not belong to the council of my people or be listed in the records of the house of Israel, nor will they enter the land of Israel. Then you will know that I am the Sovereign* LORD. "'Because they lead my people*

astray, saying, "Peace," when there is no peace, and because, when a flimsy wall is built, they cover it with whitewash (Ezekiel 13:2–10).

Once again the Lord warns those who prophesy not to do so out of their own imagination. In other words, do not go beyond what is written and don't add anything to what God has said. **If God did not say it, then we are not to proclaim it.** Notice that the Lord indicates in this passage that the false prophets actually expect their prophecies to come true. This means that the prophet's sincerity and conviction are no guarantees that their prophecy is true. Only through a careful examination of the Word are false prophecies revealed.

The Lord also has some advice for His people as well. Let's see what the Lord says through Isaiah.

Go now, write it on a tablet for them, ***inscribe it on a scroll, that for the days to come it may be an everlasting witness.*** *These are rebellious people, deceitful children, children unwilling to listen to the* LORD's *instruction. They say to the seers, "See no more visions!" and to the prophets, "Give us no more visions of what is right! Tell us pleasant things, prophesy illusions. Leave this way, get off this path, and stop confronting us with the Holy One of Israel!" Therefore, this is what the Holy One of Israel says: "Because you have rejected this message, relied on oppression and depended on deceit, this sin will become for you like a high wall, cracked and bulging, that collapses suddenly, in an instant* (Isaiah 30:8–13).

Isaiah records that we have the written Word of God as *"an everlasting witness,"* which is written down *"for the days to come,"* so we can read and understand what God has said and what He didn't say.

Finally, God has also spoken to the shepherds of His flock, regarding the last days:

> *Woe to the shepherds of Israel who only take care of themselves! Should not shepherds take care of the flock? You eat the curds, clothe yourselves with the wool and slaughter the choice animals, but you do not take care of the flock. You have not strengthened the weak or healed the sick or bound up the injured. You have not brought back the strays or searched for the lost. You have ruled them harshly and brutally..." Therefore, you shepherds, hear the word of the* LORD: *...because my shepherds did not search for my flock but cared for themselves rather than for my flock, therefore, ...I am against the shepherds and will hold them accountable for my flock* (Ezekiel 34:2–9).

The prophets gave us clear descriptions of the last days' events, along with important spiritual warnings which we would be wise to take to heart and put into practice.

CHAPTER EIGHT

Revelation of Jesus Christ

The revelation of Jesus Christ,
which God gave him to show his servants
what must soon take place (Revelation 1:1).

The Apostle John received the Revelation from Jesus Christ to show His servants what will soon take place. We know that the Revelation is primarily about the last days because its content is extensively connected to their events.

John says the Revelation is about *"what must soon take place,"* and he uses the word "soon" eight times in the Revelation to describe the events of the last days and the "soon" return of Christ.

Correctly interpreting the Book of Revelation presents a formidable challenge to students of the Bible and can only be managed when the scriptural references and biblical patterns are understood. A good example of a scriptural pattern is seen in the Olivet Discourse. In the Olivet Discourse (Matthew 24), Jesus moves back and forth in time as He describes the events of the last days. This pattern requires the student to pay close attention to the details of what Jesus is describing. Both the Olivet Discourse and Revelation are descriptions of the last days, and Jesus Christ gave both. While the interpretation of Revelation is challenging, it is important to remember that it was given to the followers of Christ to understand and apply to our lives.

To ensure our being mindful of what He is showing us, Jesus provides a special blessing for those who read it and for those who hear it and take to heart the His words. There is no other book of Scripture that carries such a promise. Christ may have provided this additional incentive to encourage our efforts, knowing that the book requires careful study. However, it is more likely that this blessing is an indication of the importance of the Revelation for the Church.

The goal of our study of Revelation is to provide insight into the events of the last days, not to explain every detail of the prophecy.

■ INTRODUCTION

As the Book of Revelation opens, John is instructed to write what he sees and send it to seven churches in Asia: Ephesus, Smyrna, Pergamum, Thyatira, Sardis, Philadelphia and Laodicea. Then he is told the mystery relating to the seven churches which we see here in these verses.

> *The mystery of the seven stars that you saw in my right hand and of the seven golden lampstands is this:* **The seven stars are the angels of the seven churches,** *and the seven lampstands are the seven churches* (Revelation 1:20).

We see in verse 13 that Jesus is among the churches and exercising authority over the seven angels of the churches.

> ...among the lampstands was someone "like a son
> of man," dressed in a robe reaching down to his feet
> and with a golden sash around his chest. ...In his
> right hand he held seven stars (Revelation 1:13,16).

That "*the angels*" are in the right hand of Jesus is an
indication of His authority over the Church. As Jesus is at
the right hand of the Father in Heaven, the seven angels
are in Christ's right hand. Notice, also, that when John
writes the letters, they are addressed to the seven angels of
the churches, not the seven churches in Asia. Therefore,
we should conclude from what is written that the letters
are written to the whole Church, not just these seven specific churches.

With regard to Christ's responsibility and authority over
the Church, we have been told, in Hebrews 4:14, that Jesus
is our "*high priest*." From the Old Testament we also
understand that it is the high priest's responsibility to care
for the temple, including the lampstands. We also know that
Christ cares for the whole Church—not just seven churches.

So, what is meant by the reference to seven churches?
Here, as in other places in Scripture, the number "seven" represents completeness, which means that the "seven" angels
care for all of Christ's Church, which is the Body of Christ.

Therefore, not only was the Revelation written for the
seven churches in Asia, but also for the whole Church from
the time of Christ's departure until His return. This is borne
out as we read the letters and find the timeless and spiritual
nature of their message. Their message can be read with
understanding and application by the households of God as
well as by its individual members. Let's look and see what
Christ says to the angels of the churches as He cares for the
Church and prepares her for the last days.

■ REVELATION 2 AND 3—
LETTERS TO THE ANGELS OF THE CHURCHES

Jesus instructs those who are watching and waiting for His return to persevere in the faith. He reminds us that we are to remain spiritually alert and not to be distracted by the cares of this life and the deceitfulness of wealth. We must turn from sin and be obedient to Him, or we will not see the day approaching.

> *Only hold on to what you have until I come. To him who overcomes and does my will to the end, I will give authority over the nations* (Revelation 2:25,26).

> *Remember, therefore, what you have received and heard; obey it, and repent. But if you do not wake up, I will come like a thief, and you will not know at what time I will come to you* (Revelation 3:3).

Jesus uses the expression, *"I will come like a thief,"* regarding His coming. The apostle Paul also used the same expression in describing the coming of Jesus Christ on the Day of the Lord. In each case, the expression *"will come like a thief"* is used to emphasize the need for spiritual alertness and watchfulness on the part of the followers of Christ. Remember how Paul contrasted the believers to the people of the world, when he said **that day would not surprise the believers** like a thief.

As we learned earlier, the warning to be spiritually alert is repeated often throughout Scripture. Revelation is no exception. Jesus encourages us to patiently endure:

> *Since you have kept my command to endure patiently, I will also keep you from the hour of trial*

that is going to come upon the whole world to test those who live on the earth (Revelation 3:10).

This time of trial and testing that is coming on the whole world is most likely the Great Tribulation, when the Antichrist will reign over the whole world.

Some people have been told this verse indicates that the Church will be removed from the earth before the Great Tribulation. When we test this theory by the Word, we find it does not stand the test of Scripture. For example, the Holy Spirit consistently instructs believers in the Word of God that they must be prepared to face tribulation and persecution. Therefore, to assume that believers are removed from the earth before the Great Tribulation is contradictory to what is written in the Word.

Once again we find that the Greek helps us to correctly [understand what the] Lord *is* saying in this verse and what [it is not. Let us] examine the Greek in this text as we

[Since you have ke]*pt* [tereo] *my command to endure* [patiently, I will] *keep* [tereo] *you from* [ek] *the hour* [that is going] *to come upon the whole world to* [test those who live] *on the earth* (Revelation 3:10).

[Here are the def]initions for the Greek word *tereo*.

[To] guard (from loss or injury by keeping [the eye upon . . . t]o keep unmarried):—hold fast, keep (-[er, reserv]e) serve, watch.[1]

[T]o attend to carefully, take care of, to [keep] one in that state in which he is.[2]

[There is no indi]cation of removal in either of these [definitions. On the] contrary, *tereo* actually means to

guard or watch over a person, in his or her current state.

The other pertinent Greek word in this text is *ek*. *Ek* is a very common Greek word and is used over 800 times in the New Testament. It is translated twenty-five different ways in the *King James Version* of the Bible, including: among, at, because of, by, from, of, on, out of, and with.[3]

We have already seen that *tereo* can mean "kept within the sphere of." When *tereo* and *ek* are used together, they still mean, "to keep or to guard within the sphere of." However, the best way to determine the true meaning of this verse is to have Scripture interpret Scripture. Since these two Greek words are common in the New Testament, how can we accomplish this with certainty? In this case, we are indeed fortunate. As it turns out, **there is only one other place in the entire New Testament where tereo and ek are used together** and the Apostle John is also the writer. John also used this combination of words—*tereo ek*—to record Jesus' prayer for the disciples. Let's see how John uses *tereo ek* in this verse: *"My prayer is not that you take them out of the world but that you protect* [tereo] *them from* [ek] *the evil one"* (John 17:15).

Not only does John's usage clearly show the intended meaning of *tereo ek*, but Jesus' prayer actually states that the believers will be protected from Satan as they remain in the world. This idea is further confirmed in Revelation 7:3, when we see the servants of God being sealed for protection before the seven trumpets are sounded. Then we see that those sealed are protected from the locusts of the fifth trumpet (Revelation 9:4).

There is still one more passage of Scripture which will help us correctly understand the use of *tereo*. Paul used *tereo* when indicating that the Church would be kept spiritually until the Lord's return. Once again, the meaning of *tereo* means "to protect within the sphere of"—not removal.

May God himself, the God of peace, sanctify you through and through. May your whole spirit, soul and body be kept [tereo] *blameless at the coming of our Lord Jesus Christ* (1 Thessalonians 5:23).

Letting Scripture interpret Scripture, we find that, in Revelation 3:10, the believers will be protected as they go through the Great Tribulation. Therefore, while some people tell us Revelation 3:10 gives support for a Pre-Tribulation Rapture, the Word of God provides none!

■ REVELATION 4—
VISION OF THE THRONE IN HEAVEN

After the letters to the angels of the seven churches, John describes his vision of God's heavenly throne:

After this I looked, and there before me was a door standing open in heaven. And the voice I had first heard speaking to me like a trumpet said, "Come up here, and I will show you what must take place after this." At once I was in the Spirit, and there before me was a throne in heaven with someone sitting on it... Surrounding the throne were twenty-four other thrones, and seated on them were twenty-four elders (Revelation 4:1–4).

John was not the first person to receive a vision of the heavenly throne. Several times in the Old Testament, we are told of the heavenly throne. Also, in 2 Corinthians 12:2–4, Paul tells of a time when he was caught up to heaven. Paul heard things that he was not permitted to reveal. But John was caught up to heaven for the express purpose of revealing to the Church what he saw. He describes the throne of God surrounded by the twenty-four elders and the four living creatures.

There are several other references to the heavenly throne and the heavenly host in the Scripture. Here are a couple of examples—

The LORD has established his throne in heaven, and his kingdom rules over all. Praise the LORD, you his angels, you mighty ones who do his bidding, who obey his word. Praise the LORD, all his heavenly hosts, you his servants who do his will (Psalm 103:19–21).

"Suddenly a great company of the heavenly host appeared with the angel, praising God and saying..." (Luke 2:13).

The twenty-four elders and the four living creatures are part of the heavenly host. Notice when the twenty-four elders make proclamations, they refer to the saints of God as a group distinct from themselves. Read these examples to see how they refer to the saints as "*they*," "*their*" and "*them*."

You are worthy, our LORD and God, to receive glory and honor and power, for you created all things, and by your will **they** *were created and have* **their** *being* (Revelation 4:11).

"You have made **them** *to be a kingdom and priests to serve our God, and* **they** *will reign on the earth"* (Revelation 5:10).

This supports the idea that there is a heavenly host which has existed and continues to exist in heaven. We know from what is written that the Father has His throne in heaven and the Son will have His throne on earth. For example, "*At that time they will call Jerusalem The Throne of the LORD, and all nations will gather in Jerusalem to honor the name of the LORD* (Jeremiah 3:17); "*To him who overcomes, I will give the right to sit with me on my throne, just as I overcame and sat down with my Father on his throne*" (Revelation 3:21).

■ REVELATION 5—
THE SEVEN-SEALED SCROLL

As John is viewing the heavenly throne, he tells us about the scroll with seven seals that is in the right hand of God.

> *Then I saw in the right hand of him who sat on the throne a scroll with writing on both sides and sealed with seven seals. And I saw a mighty angel proclaiming in a loud voice, "Who is worthy to break the seals and open the scroll?" ...Then one of the elders said to me, "Do not weep! See, the Lion of the tribe of Judah, the Root of David, has triumphed. He is able to open the scroll and its seven seals"* (Revelation 5:1–5).

The contents of the scroll must be extremely important, because when John believes that no one is found who is worthy to open it, he weeps and weeps until he is told by one of the elders that Christ is able to open the scroll and reveal its contents.

■ REVELATION 6—
OPENING OF THE FIRST SIX SEALS

As the seals of the scroll are opened, John sees a sequence of events that will affect earth in the last days. As the first four seals are opened, they reveal four horses and their riders. When each seal is opened, the rider and horse are told to "*Come!*" John then describes what happens on the earth as each has its effect. There appears to be some connection between the heavenly scene of the horses and riders coming forth and the earthly consequences. However, based on what is written, it is impossible to understand how these things are connected. The significance of these horses and riders has been debated and spec-ulated about for centuries and it is unlikely that we can resolve this mystery in our study.

This prophecy, like various others, is most likely given to us so we will see the sovereign hand of God in its fulfill-ment, not so we can predict the future. However, as we con-sider these things, we would be remiss if we didn't review the Scripture which appears to be related to these events.

First, as we review the scriptural record, we find that the Jewish people referred to Pharaoh and his army as *"the horse and its rider"*—

> *Then Moses and the Israelites sang this song to the* LORD: *"I will sing to the* LORD, *for he is highly exalted.* **The horse** and **its rider** *he has hurled into the sea. The* LORD *is my strength and my song; he has become my salvation. He is my God, and I will praise him, my father's God, and I will exalt him. The* LORD *is a warrior; the* LORD *is his name. Pharaoh's chariots and his army he has hurled into the sea* (Exodus 15:1–4).

The horse represented the people—the army of Egypt—and the rider—Pharaoh, their leader. If this analogy holds true in the Revelation vision, it could mean that the horses will represent certain countries and the riders their leaders.

In the prophecies of Zechariah, we also find horses of different colors described in connection with the things that are taking place on earth. Perhaps we may gain insight from these prophecies as we consider the four horses of Revelation. When Zechariah inquired regarding the horses he saw in his vision, this is what he was told:

> 'They are the ones the LORD has sent to go
> throughout the earth.' And they reported to the
> angel of the LORD, who was standing among the
> myrtle trees, 'We have gone throughout the earth
> and found the whole world at rest and in peace'
> (Zechariah 1:10).

There is another vision in which Zechariah describes horses of four colors. The colors of these four horses may even match the four colors of the four horses in Revelation. These horses are said to be the four spirits of heaven, which go out to the four points of the earth.

> The first chariot had red horses, the second black, the
> third white, and the fourth dappled—all of them
> powerful. I asked the angel who was speaking to me,
> 'What are these, my lord?' The angel answered me,
> 'These are the four spirits of heaven, going out from
> standing in the presence of the Lord of the whole
> world. The one with the black horses is going toward
> the north country, the one with the white horses
> toward the west, and the one with the dappled horses
> toward the south' (Zechariah 6:2–6).

There is still another aspect to consider as we attempt to determine the meaning of the four horses and their riders. When will they ride? As we consider this question, we can't help but notice the similarities between the first four seals and what Jesus called the beginning of the birth pains in the Olivet Discourse. In both cases, Jesus is the one describing what will take place in the last days. Let's compare the two passages to see the similarities:

Matthew 24:7–14	Revelation 6:4–17
Nation rise against nation	*Peace will be taken from the earth*
and kingdom against kingdom	*and men will slay each other*
There will be famines and earth quakes in various places	*A quart of wheat for a days wages and killing by sword, famine, plague*
You will be persecuted and killed because of me and many will turn from the faith	*Those slain were told to wait until... their fellow servants which were to be killed was completed*
The end will come	*The day of their wrath has come*

Both of these passages seem to take us from the beginning of the birth pains up to the very end of the age.

When do the birth pains begin, in relation to Daniel's seventieth week? Do they begin before the seventieth week, as the Antichrist is rising to power? Do the birth pains begin at the beginning of the seven years, when the Antichrist confirms the covenant? Or do the birth pains begin in the middle of the seven years, when the Antichrist is revealed? If we can answer these questions from what is stated in the Scripture, we will know when the birth pains begin and the first seals are opened. If not, we must wait until the prophecies are fulfilled, in the future.

Now, let's look as the seals are opened. "*I looked, and there before me was a white horse! Its rider held a bow, and he was given a crown, and he rode out as a conqueror bent on conquest*" (Revelation 6:2). Some have interpreted the rider on the white horse to be Christ and a representation of the victory of the gospel. This appears to be out of place when considering the context of the four horses and their riders.

Also, when we compare this rider and white horse with Christ and the white horse in Revelation 19, we find the timing of their appearances is different. While there are passages in Scripture which seem to identify the first rider as the Antichrist, the passages are only inferences and do not clearly reveal his identity. Therefore, we must wait until the prophecies are fulfilled before we can know for certain the identity of the first rider, if indeed we will ever know the rider's identity. Remember, the riders—like their horses—may signify the four spirits of heaven and may not be earthly beings at all. To understand the meaning and the timing of these first seals, and the beginning of the birth pains, we will most likely have to wait for their fulfillment.

The idea that many Bible prophecies will require their fulfillment to reveal their truth was also the position of Sir Isaac Newton. This is what he said in his book, *Observations Upon The Prophecies of Daniel and the Apocalypse of St. John*:

> The folly of interpreters has been, to foretell times and things by this prophesy, as if God designed to make them prophets. By this rashness they have not only exposed themselves, but have brought the prophecy also into contempt. The design of God was much otherwise. He gave this and prophecies of the Old Testament, not to gratify men's curiosities by enabling then to foreknow things, but that after they were fulfilled they might be interpreted by the event, and his own Providence...[4]

While we cannot decipher everything that the Book of Revelation foretells, we should also remember that the Revelation was given to show the servants of God the things which would soon come to pass. Therefore, we will press on to understand the truth, trusting that God will reveal what He intends.

Following the white horse and its rider, a red horse and its rider are given power to take peace from the earth:

> *When the Lamb opened the second seal, I heard the second living creature say, 'Come!' Then another horse came out, a fiery red one. Its rider was given power to take peace from the earth and to make men slay each other. To him was given a large sword* (Revelation 6:3,4).

Prior to the red horse and its rider, the world may be in relative peace. Relative, because there will always be wars and rumors of wars. However, once the red horse comes on the scene, war and killing will become worldwide. This rider is given a large sword, a term often used in Scripture to symbolize military power. Notice its use here in Isaiah: "*Nation will not take up sword against nation, nor will they train for war anymore*" (Isaiah 2:4).

Following the red horse and its rider is a black horse and its rider. This horse and rider bring what would seem to be the inevitable result of the worldwide wars. The wars will have caused incredible devastation to the world's ecology and food production, resulting in severe shortages. These food shortages will make today's food production and distribution problems pale in comparison:

> *When the Lamb opened the third seal, I heard the third living creature say, 'Come!' I looked, and there*

before me was a black horse! Its rider was holding a pair of scales in his hand. Then I heard what sounded like a voice among the four living creatures, saying, 'A quart of wheat for a day's wages, and three quarts of barley for a day's wages, and do not damage the oil and the wine!' (Revelation 6:5,6).

The fourth seal is the last in the series of horses and riders. The rider on the pale horse appears to bring either a natural conclusion of the previous three horses or to be a consummation of the first three. The image presented is not new; God used the sword, famine and plague to chastise and warn Israel to repent and turn back to God. Here, God may once again be employing the sword, famine, plague and wild beasts in the last days for the same purpose. In this vision, we see that the rider's influence is over one quarter of the earth:

When the Lamb opened the fourth seal, I heard the voice of the fourth living creature say, 'Come!' I looked, and there before me was a pale horse! Its rider was named Death, and Hades was following close behind him. They were given power over a fourth of the earth to kill by sword, famine and plague, and by the wild beasts of the earth (Revelation 6:7,8).

So that we have a perspective of this concept of *"sword, famine, plague and wild beast,"* let's see how God employed these in the past. The writing of Jeremiah and Ezekiel may help us understand how these things will be used by God in the last days leading up to the return of Christ.

Then the LORD said to me, 'Do not pray for the well-being of this people. ...Instead, I will destroy them with the sword, famine and plague.' But I said, Ah, Sovereign LORD, *the prophets keep telling them, 'You will not see the sword or suffer famine. Indeed, I will give you lasting peace in this place.' Then the* LORD *said to me, 'The prophets are prophesying lies in my name. I have not sent them or appointed them or spoken to them'* (Jeremiah 14:11–14).

Or if I send a plague into that land and pour out my wrath upon it through bloodshed, killing its men and their animals... For this is what the Sovereign LORD *says: How much worse will it be when I send against Jerusalem my four dreadful judgments—* **sword and famine and wild beasts and plague***—to kill its men and their animals! Yet there will be some survivors* (Ezekiel 14:19–22).

If we continue to follow Jesus' outline in the Olivet Discourse for understanding the Book of Revelation, then we would expect to see more indications of the Great Tribulation. According to Jesus, in Matthew 24, this severe persecution will cause many to turn away from the faith as they consider death or life under the Antichrist.

Then you will be handed over to be persecuted and put to death, and you will be hated by all nations because of me. At that time many will turn away from the faith and will betray and hate each other, and many false prophets will appear and deceive many people (Matthew 24:9–11).

Just as expected, we find the same thing revealed in the Revelation as we saw previously in the Olivet Discourse— the death and martyrdom of the saints.

When he opened the fifth seal, I saw under the altar the souls of those who had been slain because of the Word of God and the testimony they had maintained. They called out in a loud voice, 'How long, Sovereign Lord, holy and true, until you judge the inhabitants of the earth and avenge our blood?' Then each of them was given a white robe, and they were told to wait a little longer, until the number of their fellow servants and brothers who were to be killed as they had been was completed (Revelation 6:9–11).

The opening of the fifth seal reveals the saints who have died because of their testimony and the Word of God. These probably are the saints who have died through the ages up to this time. They almost certainly include some who have already been martyred during the Great Tribulation. However, they cannot be all the saints martyred during the Great Tribulation, because there are still others that will be killed as they had been. They are told to wait until their full number has been completed.

I watched as he opened the sixth seal. There was a great earthquake. The sun turned black like sackcloth made of goat hair, the whole moon turned blood red, and the stars in the sky fell to earth, as late figs drop from a fig tree when shaken by a strong wind. The sky receded like a scroll, rolling up, and every mountain and island was removed from its place. Then the kings of the earth, the princes, the generals, the rich, the mighty, and every slave and every free man hid in caves and among the rocks of the mountains. They called to the mountains and the rocks, 'Fall on us and hide us from the face of him who sits on the throne

and from the wrath of the Lamb! For the great day of
their wrath has come, and who can stand?'
(Revelation 6:12–17).

Just as Jesus stated in Matthew 24:29, the sun, moon
and stars will be darkened before the coming of the Son of
Man. When these signs begin to occur, the people of the
world will know that the judgment and wrath of God are at
hand. These signs in the heavens and on the earth will indicate the imminent return of the Son of Man. The passage
stops just short of Christ's return and the Day of the Lord.

If the text followed in chronological order, we would
expect to next see the appearance of the Son of Man in the
clouds. However, that is not what happens; the progression
abruptly stops and we are given a view of something that
occurred earlier. This is a common pattern in biblical
prophecy, to move back and forth covering the same ground
again. Jesus did this in the Olivet Discourse when He brought
us up to the end of the age in verse 14. Then, in verse 15, He
takes us back and provides details regarding the *abomination
that causes desolation* and the Great Tribulation. Then, once
again, He brings us to the end of the age in verse 31. What we
are observing here in Revelation is the same pattern. The
prophecy moves back and forth, first revealing a sequence of
events and then going back to provide additional details. Our
awareness of this characteristic of biblical prophecy will help
us avoid the errors caused by trying to interpret Revelation as
strictly chronological.

This brings us to the end of Revelation chapter 6, and
the Lord has brought us up to the last day at the very close
of the Great Tribulation. In keeping with the biblical pattern, the prophecy now moves back to the start of the
Great Tribulation.

■ REVELATION 7—
SPIRITUAL ISRAEL IS SEALED

John relays the vision of what will take place just before the angels sound their trumpets:

> *After this I saw four angels standing at the four corners of the earth, holding back the four winds of the earth to prevent any wind from blowing on the land or on the sea or on any tree. Then I saw another angel coming up from the east, having the seal of the living God. He called out in a loud voice to the four angels who had been given power to harm the land and the sea: 'Do not harm the land or the sea or the trees until we put a seal on the foreheads of the servants of our God'* (Revelation 7:1–3).

The four angels are told not to harm the land or the sea or the trees until the servants of God are sealed. Then, in Revelation 8, we see that destruction will fall on the earth and the sea as the first four angels sound their trumpets. When angels begin to sound their trumpets, the land and the sea will experience the fury of Satan. Satan's fury will commence when he is thrown down to earth, exactly as written here.

> *Therefore rejoice, you heavens and you who dwell in them! But woe to the earth and the sea, because the devil has gone down to you! He is filled with fury, because he knows that his time is short"* (Revelation 12:12).

However, before Satan is cast down to the earth, we see that the servants of God have already been sealed. The seal of God provides spiritual protection, guarding them during the time of trial that is coming on the whole world. We will see an example of this protection when the locusts—demons—are released from the Abyss at the fifth trumpet, Revelation 9:4. The locusts are not able to harm God's servants, because they were sealed before the Great Tribulation.

Who are these servants of God, who are sealed? Are they the Church of Jesus Christ (spiritual Israel, all believers Jewish and non-Jewish), or are they the representatives of national Israel?

Some believe this group is national Israel, because twelve tribes are named. However, this does not fit with what is written. For example, if the 144,000 represents the Jewish remnant who come to the knowledge of the Lord only at the very end of the age, then who are those who are protected as they resist the Antichrist during the Great Tribulation? Those who resist the Antichrist and hold to the testimony of Jesus Christ are the Church who have been sealed by God (Revelation 12:17; 14:12).

Who, then, are the 144,000 servants of God? In order to correctly interpret this passage, we need to understand the new covenant made by the sacrifice of Jesus Christ on the cross of Calvary. In the opening chapters of Revelation, John contrasts national Jews with spiritual Jews—the Body of Christ: *"I know your afflictions and your poverty—yet you are rich! I know the slander of those who say they are Jews and are not, but are a synagogue of Satan"* (Revelation 2:9).

> *I will make those who are of the synagogue of Satan, who claim to be Jews though they are not, but are liars—I will make them come and fall down at your feet and acknowledge that I have loved you* (Revelation 3:9).

These passages contrast national Israel and the law with spiritual Israel and the new covenant made by the blood of Christ. God has revealed through the apostles that the new covenant that He made in His blood is with His people, spiritual Israel, Jewish and non-Jewish alike. Once, God worked through the Jewish people, but now, under the new covenant, God works through all believers. These next passages make this truth abundantly clear.

> ... *a man is a* [spiritual] *Jew if he is one inwardly; and circumcision is circumcision of the heart, by the Spirit, not by the written code* (Romans 2:29).

> *This mystery is that through the gospel the Gentiles are heirs together with Israel, members together of one body, and sharers together in the promise in Christ Jesus* (Ephesians 3:6).

> *For it is we* [the Church] *who are the circumcision* [Israel], *we who worship by the Spirit of God, who glory in Christ Jesus, and who put no confidence in the flesh* (Philippians 3:3).

Therefore, there is no doubt that spiritual Israel is made up of all who believe in Jesus Christ—Jewish and non-Jewish. With this understanding of the new covenant in Christ Jesus, we can plainly see that the 144,000 servants of God represent spiritual Israel, the true Church. We also find additional support for this position in Revelation 14, when John says the 144,000 are with Christ on Mount Zion. When Christ is on Mount Zion, as we have previously seen, the Kingdom has come and the whole Church, the Bride of Christ, is with Him. This is further confirmation that the 144,000 represent all believers: "*Then I looked, and there before me was the Lamb, standing on Mount Zion, and*

with him 144,000 who had his name and his Father's name
written on their foreheads" (Revelation 14:1).

This confirms that the 144,000 are the Church, because
they are described using characteristics which exclusively
belong to the Church. Let's see how John describes the
Church:

> *These are those who did not defile themselves with*
> *women, for they kept themselves **pure**. They follow*
> *the Lamb wherever he goes. They were purchased*
> *from among men and offered as **firstfruits** to God*
> *and the Lamb* (Revelation 14:4).

We find that Paul and James use these same characteristics in describing the Church. Paul says the Church is a
"pure" virgin bride who will be presented to Christ. James
tells us that the Church is a kind of *"first fruits"* of all God
has created: *"He chose to give us birth through the word of*
truth, that we [the Church] *might be a kind of **first fruits** of*
all he created" (James 1:18); *"I am jealous for you with a*
godly jealousy. I promised you to one husband, to Christ, so
that I might present you [the Church] *as a **pure** virgin to him*
(2 Corinthians 11:2).

Therefore, based on what is written, we can see that the
144,000 servants of God represent the Church. For the
Church is spiritual Israel, *"pure"* and undefiled, a kind of
"first fruits" of all He created. After the 144,000 had been
sealed, John saw *"a great multitude"* in heaven, as he
describes here:

> *After this I looked and there before me was **a great***
> ***multitude** that no one could count, from every*
> *nation, tribe, people and language, standing before*
> *the throne and in front of the Lamb. They were*

wearing white robes and were holding palm branches in their hands. ...And he said, "These are they who have come out of the great tribulation; they have washed their robes and made them white in the blood of the Lamb (Revelation 7:9,14).

John is told that these are the martyred saints who have come out of the Great Tribulation. They are before the throne in heaven, not yet before the throne on earth. We know they are in heaven because, when John addresses one of the heavenly elders, the elder tells John what is about to happen. The elder says the Lamb *"will spread His tent over them," "will lead them to springs of living water"* and *"will wipe away every tear from their eye."* Each of these statements indicates things that will happen when Christ establishes His Kingdom.

Therefore, in this vision we first saw the Church on earth sealed before the Great Tribulation. Then, at the end of the Great Tribulation, we see the great multitude readied in heaven for the return of Christ and the resurrection of believers. Once again we are poised at the very end of the age. So, what happens next?

■ REVELATION 8—
THE SCROLL IS OPENED

What is about to happen is the most important event in John's heavenly vision—the opening of the seventh seal. The opening of the seventh seal will allow the contents of the scroll to be revealed. *"When he opened the seventh seal, there was silence in heaven for about half an hour"* (Revelation 8:1).

The contents of the scroll are so extremely important that, in the midst of these magnificent events, everything in heaven stops and there is silence for about a half-hour. A half-hour of silence in heaven at this point would seem like an eternity. Earlier, in Revelation 5, John wept and wept because he thought no one was found worthy to open the scroll. The contents of the scroll are of such great importance that all creation is waiting for its contents to be revealed. Perhaps this verse captures the importance: *"The creation waits in eager expectation for the **sons of God** to be revealed"* (Romans 8:19).

No one but Christ Himself is worthy and able to open the scroll and reveal who are the *"sons of God,"* the Church and spiritual Israel. Let's take a look at what is written as we consider the possibility that the scroll is actually the book of life.

First, let's consult the original languages for insight. The Hebrew word *sepher*[5] and the Greek word *biblos*[6] are each translated interchangeably in the Scripture as *"scroll"* and *"book."* Therefore, it is equally correct to refer to the *book of life* as the *scroll of life*. Let's look at an example from the prophecies of Daniel.

> *But at that time your people—everyone whose name is found written in the book* [sepher]*—will be delivered. Multitudes who sleep in the dust of the earth will awake: some to everlasting life, others to shame and everlasting contempt. Those who are wise will shine like the brightness of the heavens, and those who lead many to righteousness, like the stars for ever and ever. But you, Daniel, close up and seal the words* [dabar] *of the scroll* [sepher] *until the time of the end* (Daniel 12:1–4).

Not only is *sepher* used interchangeably for *"scroll"* and *"book"* in Daniel 12, but *dabar* can also be translated as "names."[7] Therefore, if we consider the context of this passage in Daniel 12:4 we see it can also make sense to translate it as, "But you, Daniel, close up and seal the names of the book until the time of the end."

While this is merely a theory, it could explain the significance placed on the scroll in the right hand of Him who sits on the throne. It is impossible to substantiate by Scripture and should not be considered more than a theory. We all long to know the names that are written in the book of life which Christ will reveal on the Day of the Lord. And since the prophecies of Daniel and the Book of Revelation reveal the events of the last days, it seems likely that something else may be contained in the scroll. The contents of the scroll have not been revealed to us, so there is nothing that allows us to confirm whether or not this *is* the book of life.

Summary of the seven seals

Let's review what John saw in the vision of the seals. The events of the first four seals seem to correspond with events Jesus described as the birth pains in the Olivet Discourse. The fifth seal brings us to the martyrdom of the saints, which we know will be unprecedented during the Great Tribulation. The sixth seal reveals the signs in the heavens and on the earth that take place just prior to the coming of the Son of Man at the end of the age. Then just before the seventh seal is opened, we are taken back to the beginning of the Great Tribulation and shown the sealing of the servants of God. After the Great Tribulation, the great multitude is readied and the seventh seal of the scroll is opened.

As we prepare to examine the seven trumpets of Revelation, it would be helpful for us to have a basic understanding of the seven Jewish feasts. God commanded Israel, in Leviticus 23, to observe seven feasts. God gave Israel the feasts to show them what was to come at the appointed times. In fact **feast in Hebrew means appointed time**. When the Messiah (Christ) came during His First Advent, He fulfilled four of the seven feasts as prescribed by God. For example, when Christ made His sacrifice on the cross of Calvary, He fulfilled in Himself the feast of Passover. Then, when Jesus was resurrected from the dead, He fulfilled the feast of First Fruits. After His ascension into heaven, when He sent the Holy Spirit to indwell the Church, He fulfilled the feast of Pentecost. Therefore, Christ has already fulfilled the first four feasts as appointed by God.

The three remaining feasts are *harvest* feasts and have yet to be fulfilled by Christ. We will see, as we study Revelation, that Christ at His Second Coming will fulfill the three *harvest* feasts. Below is a brief outline of the seven feasts, which God has given to show us what is to happen at the appointed time.

The Feasts of the Lord

	FEAST	SIGNIFICANCE
First Month		
14th day	Passover	Church is Redeemed
15th day	Unleavened Bread	Church is Cleansed
16th day	First Fruits	Christ is Raised
Third Month		
6th day	Weeks	Holy Spirit is Given
Seventh Month		
1st day	Trumpets	Church is Gathered
10th day	Atonement	Church is Judged
15th day	Tabernacles	Christ/Church United

The next feast to be fulfilled at God's appointed time is

the Feast of Trumpets. Let's examine what is written regarding the fulfillment of the Feast of Trumpets:

> *The first angel sounded his trumpet, and there came hail and fire mixed with blood, and it was hurled down upon the earth. A third of the earth was burned up, a third of the trees were burned up, and all the green grass was burned up. The second angel sounded his trumpet, and something like a huge mountain, all ablaze, was thrown into the sea. A third of the sea turned into blood, a third of the living creatures in the sea died, and a third of the ships were destroyed. The third angel sounded his trumpet, and a great star, blazing like a torch, fell from the sky on a third of the rivers and on the springs of water—the name of the star is Wormwood. A third of the waters turned bitter, and many people died from the waters that had become bitter. The fourth angel sounded his trumpet, and a third of the sun was struck, a third of the moon, and a third of the stars, so that a third of them turned dark. A third of the day was without light, and also a third of the night* (Revelation 8:7–12).

As we read what will happen during the sounding of the first four trumpets, we observe that they primarily affect the earth and the sea. This appears be a time of tremendous turmoil in the world and great destruction of the earth, the sea and the environment. This destruction in the earth and sea seems connected to a subsequent passage, in Revelation 12, when the archangel Michael throws Satan to earth.

> *And there was war in heaven. Michael and his angels fought against the dragon, and the dragon*

and his angels fought back. But he was not strong enough, and they lost their place in heaven. The great dragon was hurled down—that ancient serpent called the devil, or Satan, who leads the whole world astray. He was hurled to the earth, and his angels with him (Revelation 12:7–9).

The reason these two passages seem connected is because when Satan is thrown down to the earth, he immediately brings destruction on the earth and sea:

Therefore rejoice, you heavens and you who dwell in them! But woe to the earth and the sea, because the devil has gone down to you! He is filled with fury, because he knows that his time is short. (Revelation 12:12).

There will be great destruction to the earth and the sea, as described in the first four trumpets, when Michael throws Satan down to the earth. Following the destruction on the earth and the sea (Revelation 8), there will be destruction and persecution affecting mankind.

■ REVELATION 9—
THE DEMONS RELEASED

As we continue with John's visions, we should remember that John was in the Spirit, which may indicate that some of what John saw are spiritual things only visible in the Spirit and not visible to the flesh.

The fifth angel sounded his trumpet, and I saw a star that had fallen from the sky to the earth. The star was given the key to the shaft of the Abyss. When he opened the Abyss, smoke rose from it like the smoke from a gigantic furnace. The sun and sky

were darkened by the smoke from the Abyss. And
out of the smoke locusts came down upon the earth
and were given power like that of scorpions of the
earth. They were told not to harm the grass of the
earth or any plant or tree, but only those people
who did not have the seal of God on their foreheads
(Revelation 9:1–4).

What John sees during the time of the trumpets may at least in part represent supernatural activity occurring in the world during the Great Tribulation. When the fifth trumpet is sounded, a star is seen which had fallen to the earth. This star may be Satan, who we know at this point during the Great Tribulation, has already been cast down to earth by Michael. If this is correct, Satan will be given the key to the Abyss and will release what appears to be an army of demons which will torment the people of the earth. When these demons come up out of the Abyss, they have as their leader an angel whose name means *destroyer*. "*They had as king over them the angel of the Abyss, whose name in Hebrew is Abaddon, and in Greek, Apollyon*" (Revelation 9:11).

We also know, from what is written in chapter 9, that the Abyss is located on the earth and, therefore, the angel of the Abyss comes out of the earth. This information will help us understand where the False Prophet comes from in Revelation 13, because we are told the False Prophet comes out of the earth.

After the demons are released, the sixth trumpet sounds and 200,000,000 troops gather from the great river Euphrates in the east; this may be part of what the Scripture refers to as the gathering of the nations in preparation for the final battle of Armageddon.

We are also told in chapter 9 that, even after all this dev-astation, those who remain in the world will not repent and turn to God:

> *The rest of mankind that were not killed by these plagues still did not repent of the work of their hands; they did not stop worshiping demons, and idols of gold, silver, bronze, stone and wood—idols that cannot see or hear or walk. Nor did they repent of their murders, their magic arts, their sexual immorality or their thefts* (Revelation 9:20,21).

■ REVELATION 10—
READY OR NOT

We should also note that in Scripture, there are two principal uses for the trumpet—one is to sound a warning and the other is to call the assembly of God's people. It appears, from what is written, that the first six trumpets in Revelation are warnings of God's coming judgment. The sixth trumpet appears to be the last call to repent, since the seventh (and last) trumpet signals the resurrection and gath-ering of all believers at the beginning of Christ's reign on earth. Following the sixth trumpet—but before the sev-enth—John tells us,

> *But in the days when the seventh angel is about to sound his trumpet, **the mystery of God will be accomplished**, just as he announced to his servants the prophets* (Revelation 10:7).

■ REVELATION 11—
TWO WITNESSES AND THE LAST TRUMPET

Here, as John is told to measure the temple, he is given two identical periods of time, "*42 months*" and "*1,260 days.*" Each of these periods equals three and a half years in the Jewish prophetic calendar.

> *I was given a reed like a measuring rod and was told, "Go and measure the temple of God and the altar, and count the worshipers there. But exclude the outer court; do not measure it, because it has been given to the Gentiles. They will trample on the holy city for 42 months. And I will give power to my two witnesses, and they will prophesy for 1,260 days, clothed in sackcloth"* (Revelation 11:1–3).

By now we should recognize this three-and-a-half-year period as the Great Tribulation. During the Great Tribulation, Gentiles (unbelievers) will have possession of the holy city, Jerusalem. Also during this period, the two witnesses of God will exercise great power as they prophesy and testify of the Lord. One of these is almost certainly Elijah, as we see written in Malachi: *"See, I will send you the prophet Elijah before that great and dreadful day of the LORD comes"* (Malachi 4:5).

The other is most likely Moses. These are the two lamp stands that stand before the Lord, just as they stood before the Lord on the Mount of Transfiguration.

> *There he was transfigured before them. His face shone like the sun, and his clothes became as white as the light. Just then there appeared before them Moses and Elijah, talking with Jesus* (Matthew 17:2,3).

At the end of the Great Tribulation, when they have finished their testimony, the beast—known as the False Prophet—will overpower and kill them. But after three and a half days, the breath of life will enter into them and they will be called up to heaven in a cloud. Then, John tells us, there will be a great earthquake in Jerusalem, which will kill 7,000 people. The survivors of the earthquake will give glory to God. Now, if all the survivors give glory to God, this may be the fulfillment of Jesus' prophecy as written in Matthew—"*For I tell you, you will not see me again until you say, 'Blessed is he who comes in the name of the Lord'*" (Matthew 24:39).

If the remnant of Jewish people recognize Jesus as Lord, this may trigger His return and the Day of the Lord. Since we know when Christ returns, all believers will be resurrected, we would expect the last trumpet to sound at this point.

The last trumpet

Just as we expected, when the seventh and last trumpet sounds in Revelation 11:15, we see the Kingdom come and the resurrection of the saints. Let's read this carefully to see all that will take place at the last trumpet:

> *The seventh angel sounded his trumpet, and there were loud voices in heaven, which said: 'The kingdom of the world has become the kingdom of our Lord and of his Christ, and he will reign for ever and ever.' And the twenty-four elders, who were seated on their thrones before God, fell on their faces and worshiped God, saying: 'We give thanks to you, Lord God Almighty, the One who is and who was, because you have taken your great power and have begun to reign. The nations were angry; and your wrath has come. The time has come for judging the dead, and for rewarding your servants the prophets and your saints and those who reverence your name, both small and great—and for destroying those who destroy the earth'* (Revelation 11:15–18).

When the last trumpet sounds:

1.   Jesus begins His reign over the Kingdom of God on earth.
2.   The resurrection of the saints occurs.
3.   The saints are judged and they receive their reward.
4.   The wrath of God is poured out on unbelievers.

From what we have read, this timeline depicts when the trumpets will sound during the last days.

Last Days Timeline

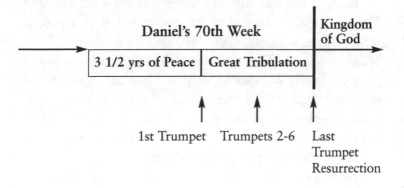

■ REVELATION 12—
A VISION OF ISRAEL

Once again it appears that the vision stops at the return of Christ, and then goes back to give us additional details to help us understand what is going to happen in the last days.

A great and wondrous sign appeared in heaven: a woman [Israel] clothed with the sun, with the moon under her feet and a crown of twelve stars on her head. She was pregnant and cried out in pain as she was about to give birth. Then another sign appeared in heaven: an enormous red dragon [Satan] with seven heads and ten horns and seven crowns on his heads [Fourth Beast Kingdom]. *His tail swept a third of the stars out of the sky and flung them to the earth. The dragon stood in front of the woman who was about to give birth, so that he might devour her child the moment it was born. She gave birth to a son, a male child* [Christ], *who will rule all the nations with an iron scepter. And her child was snatched up to God and to his throne* (Revelation 12:1–5).

Israel is the woman with the twelve stars on her head. The twelve stars represent the twelve tribes of Israel, as described in Genesis 37:9. We also know this is Israel because she gives birth to Christ, who came from the Jewish people—Israel. We also know that Satan attempted to kill the Christ child when Herod had all the young male children in Bethlehem put to death. Finally, we see that Christ is caught up to heaven, as He was in His ascension into heaven at the end of His First Advent.

Next we see how Satan loses his place in heaven.

The woman fled into the desert to a place prepared for her by God, where she might be taken care of **for 1,260 days** [three and a half years]. *And there was war in heaven. Michael and his angels fought against the dragon, and the dragon and his angels fought back. But he was not strong enough, and they lost their place in heaven. The great dragon was hurled down— that ancient serpent called the devil, or Satan* (Revelation 12:6–9).

Satan then pursues Israel, but God protects her for three and a half years of the Great Tribulation. When Satan cannot destroy all of Israel, he will make war against the saints, those who hold to the testimony of Jesus.

■ REVELATION 13—
THE TWO BEASTS

In this chapter, John describes the rise of the first beast (known as the Antichrist) and of the second beast (known as the False Prophet). *"And the dragon stood on the shore of the sea. And I saw a beast coming out of the sea. He had ten horns and seven heads, with ten crowns on his horns"* (Revelation 13:1).

The first beast is said to have ten horns and seven heads, which connects this prophecy to Daniel's prophecy of the fourth beast kingdom that will rise to world power in the last days. As we saw in Daniel, the Antichrist will come to power out of the fourth beast kingdom. Again, let's see how Daniel describes his rise to power:

> *The fourth beast is a fourth kingdom that will appear on earth. It will be different from all the other kingdoms and will devour the whole earth, trampling it down and crushing it. The ten horns are ten kings who will come from this kingdom. After them another king will arise, different from the earlier ones; he will subdue three kings* (Daniel 7:23,24).

John tells us several things about the Antichrist. He will be very successful in war, because the whole world says, who can make war against him? The Antichrist will be killed, but his fatal wound will be miraculously healed. At the peak of his career, he will go into the temple of God and declare himself to be God. Then he will make war against the saints and conquer them during the three and a half years of the Great Tribulation. His dominion will be so complete that everyone whose name is not found written in the book of life will worship the Antichrist.

Then John describes a second beast that comes out of the earth. We may recall, at the fifth trumpet, the angel from the Abyss whose name means **destroyer** also comes out of the earth. This second beast appears to assist the Antichrist in carrying out Satan's plan to destroy the people of God. The second beast is the False Prophet, who is also identified later in Revelation chapters 16, 19 and 20.

The False Prophet, we are told, will perform great signs and wonders to deceive the whole world. He will even cause fire to come down from the sky to earth in full view of men and will force everyone—from the national leaders to the common man—to worship the Antichrist and take his mark. Anyone who does not have the mark will not be able to buy or sell anything, or make any type of financial transaction. All those who refuse the mark are to be killed. The mark of the first beast is associated with the identity of the Antichrist and is connected to the number 666.

"This calls for wisdom. If anyone has insight, let him calculate the number of the beast, for it is man's number. His number is 666" (Revelation 13:18). Many people have spent a great deal of time and energy trying to determine the identity of the Antichrist by inventing various ways of calculating his number. However, as we have seen in our study, if we have a scriptural question, our first recourse should always be to search the Scripture for the answer. This passage even provides a clue to where we may find the answer. It says, *"This calls for wisdom,"* and where is wisdom obtained? The Bible reveals that wisdom comes from God—*"If any of you lacks wisdom, he should ask God"* (James 1:5). Therefore, let us turn to the Scripture

and ask God to show us how to identify the Antichrist.

Remember, when we were studying 2 Thessalonians 2:3–4, Paul told us the man of lawlessness would be revealed when he goes into the temple and declares himself to be God. Therefore, Paul is saying the Antichrist will be revealed at the *abomination that causes desolation*. Now, we may suspect that this world leader is the Antichrist before the *abomination that causes desolation*, but we will not be certain until the *abomination that causes desolation*. At that time, Paul says, we will know the identity of the Antichrist. So, what is the significance of the number 666 in Revelation?

The Scripture says, *"Every matter must be established by the testimony of two or three witnesses."*[8] Paul is one witness, and he writes that the Antichrist will be revealed at the *abomination that causes desolation*. Isaiah is the second witness, and he wrote of the same event—he describes what will happen in the temple in Jerusalem when the Antichrist declares that he is God. Now, let's read how Isaiah describes what happens next. *"Hear that uproar from the city, hear that noise from the temple! It is the sound of the LORD repaying his enemies all they deserve"* (Isaiah 66:6).

According to Isaiah, this will happen in Jerusalem at the time of the *abomination that causes desolation*. The Antichrist and his armies have surrounded the holy city (Luke 21:20) and the Antichrist has come to the Jewish temple. Then he causes the sacrifice and offering to cease and sets up the *abomination that causes desolation* (Daniel 9:27 and 2 Thessalonians 2:3,4).

When he performs this detestable act, it is very likely that the Jewish priests will become infuriated and resist him and his army. Jesus told us this would be a time of unprecedented tribulation and persecution, worse than anything since the beginning of creation. Anyone who does not accept and submit to the Antichrist will be slaughtered during the Great Tribulation (Matthew 24:21,22). The *"uproar from the city"* and the *"noise from the temple"* will be the sound of the Great Tribulation.

As we can see, Isaiah 66:6 describes what will happen in Jerusalem and the temple at the time the Antichrist is revealed. Isaiah points us, in this passage, to the identity of the Antichrist and when his identity will be known.

John also provided another clue when he said, *"the number of the beast, is man's number."* The system of numbers used to identify the chapters and verses in the Bible where placed there by man after the Bible was canonized—they are not part of the original text. Therefore, the 66:6 of Isaiah is man's number, and the biblical answer to the Revelation mystery of the number 666. Isaiah 66:6 reveals when the Antichrist will be known.

■ REVELATION 14—
THE ANGELS PROCLAIM TO THE WORLD

Once again, the vision changes and moves to the end of the age, when the Kingdom of God has come. John sees Christ standing on Mount Zion (in Jerusalem) with the Bride of Christ:

> *Then I looked, and there before me was the Lamb, standing on Mount Zion, and with him 144,000 who had his name and his Father's name written on their foreheads* (Revelation 14:1).

The elect of God (His Bride) are standing with Christ on Mount Zion. They are undefiled and pure; the redeemed of the earth, purchased from among men as first fruits to God and Christ. This scene takes place following the resurrection of believers and Christ's return to earth.

Then once again the vision moves back, to sometime before the Coming of Christ. John records three proclamations to those who live on the earth, to every nation, tribe, language and people:

> *Then I saw another angel flying in midair, and he had the eternal gospel to proclaim to those who live on the earth—to every nation, tribe, language and people. He said in a loud voice, "Fear God and give him glory, because the hour of his judgment has come. Worship him who made the heavens, the earth, the sea and the springs of water"* (Revelation 14:6,7).

Jesus told us, in Matthew 24:14, "*this gospel of the Kingdom will be preached in the whole world as a testimony to all nations, and then the end will come.*" Just as Jesus said, the first angel proclaims the gospel to the whole world. After the gospel is proclaimed, two other angels follow:

> *A second angel followed and said, 'Fallen! Fallen is Babylon the Great, which made all the nations drink the maddening wine of her adulteries.' A third angel followed them and said in a loud voice: 'If anyone worships the beast and his image and receives his mark on the forehead or on the hand, he, too, will drink of the wine of God's fury, which has been poured full strength into the cup of his wrath. He will be tormented with burning sulfur in the presence of the holy angels and of the Lamb. And the smoke of their torment rises for ever and ever. There is no rest day or night for those who worship the beast and his image, or for anyone who receives the mark of his name'* (Revelation 14:8–11).

Based on the content of these proclamations, they most likely will take place sometime during the Great Tribulation. First, we know that they all take place before the end of the age and the return of Christ (Matthew 24:14). Second, the beast and his mark do not occur until after the Antichrist is revealed at *the abomination that causes desolation*. Finally, we are told that Mystery Babylon the Great has been destroyed. Therefore, we can place these angelic announcements as made sometime during the Great Tribulation. Following these proclamations the saints are encouraged to endure to the death for their reward will follow them:

> *This calls for patient endurance on the part of the saints who obey God's commandments and remain faithful to Jesus. Then I heard a voice from heaven say, 'Write: Blessed are the dead who die in the Lord from now on.'" "Yes," says the Spirit, "they will rest from their labor, for their deeds will follow them'* (Revelation 14:12,13).

This call to remain faithful to the end is repeated throughout the gospel whenever we read of the last days. Jesus also told us that we would be called upon to give our lives for Him and the gospel. The Lord gave these instructions, which are recorded five times in the three Gospels of Matthew, Mark and Luke:

> *For whoever wants to save his life will lose it, but whoever loses his life for me and for the gospel will save it. What good is it for a man to gain the whole world, yet forfeit his soul?* (Mark 8:35,36).

The reason for our patient endurance is revealed in the next vision. John sees the Son of Man, coming on the clouds in great glory, as the *"harvest"* is described.

I looked, and there before me was a white cloud, and seated on the cloud was one "like a son of man" with a crown of gold on his head and a sharp sickle in his hand. Then another angel came out of the temple and called in a loud voice to him who was sitting on the cloud, 'Take your sickle and reap, because the time to reap has come, for the harvest of the earth is ripe.' So he who was seated on the cloud swung his sickle over the earth, and the earth was harvested. Another angel came out of the temple in heaven, and he too had a sharp sickle. Still another angel, who had charge of the fire, came from the altar and called in a loud voice to him who had the sharp sickle, 'Take your sharp sickle and gather the clusters of grapes from the earth's vine, because its grapes are ripe.' The angel swung his sickle on the earth, gathered its grapes and threw them into the great winepress of God's wrath. They were trampled in the winepress outside the city, and blood flowed out of the press, rising as high as the horses' bridles for a distance of 1,600 stadia (Revelation 14:14–20).

John not only witnesses the "*harvest*" when the Son of Man comes on the clouds, he also witnesses the judgment and defeat of His enemies at the battle of Armageddon.

■ REVELATION 15—
JUST BEFORE HIS WRATH

After the believers have been gathered to the Lord, John tells us of the preparations for the pouring out of the seven bowls of God's judgment and wrath. The seven golden bowls of God's wrath are given to the seven angels to punish the unbelievers and the disobedient.

The wrath of God being poured out, after the believers have been removed, is a spiritual principle which God has repeated throughout Scripture. He demonstrated it when Lot left Sodom before the destruction of Sodom and Gomorrah (Genesis 19), and when Noah entered the ark before the flood. Paul encouraged us on several occasions to wait for Christ who would rescue us from the wrath of God. In his first letter to the Thessalonians, Paul says, "*...and to wait for his Son from heaven, whom he raised from the dead— Jesus, who rescues us from the coming wrath*" (1 Thessalonians 1:10).

We also notice, in Revelation, that there are no saints mentioned on the earth after the last trumpet sounds. Though the saints suffer the trials of the Great Tribulation, they are not subjected to God's wrath—having already been gathered to the Lord at the "*harvest.*"

■ REVELATION 16— THE BOWLS OF GOD'S WRATH

Then John hears the command to pour out the bowls of God's wrath on the earth. Let's see how he describes the wrath of God being poured out:

> *Then I heard a loud voice from the temple saying to the seven angels, 'Go, pour out the seven bowls of God's wrath on the earth.' The first angel went and poured out his bowl on the land, and ugly and painful sores broke out on the people who had the mark of the beast and worshiped his image. The second angel poured out his bowl on the sea, and it turned into blood like that of a dead man, and every living thing in the sea died. The third angel poured out his bowl on the rivers and springs of water, and they became blood. And I heard the altar respond:*

'Yes, Lord God Almighty, true and just are your
judgments.' The fourth angel poured out his bowl
on the sun, and the sun was given power to scorch
people with fire. The fifth angel poured out his bowl
on the throne of the beast, and his kingdom was
plunged into darkness. Men gnawed their tongues in
agony and cursed the God of heaven because of
their pains and their sores, but they refused to
repent of what they had done. The sixth angel
poured out his bowl on the great river Euphrates,
and its water was dried up to prepare the way for
the kings from the East (Revelation 16:1–12).

God's wrath is poured out on the earth and on all those
who have *the mark of the beast*. We must remember: **never
take the mark of the beast**. We have been warned ahead of
time. For those who think because they were **once saved**,
that they are able to take the mark with impunity, read and
understand this Scripture!

■ REVELATION 17—
MYSTERY BABYLON AND THE WORLD

The next two chapters of Revelation give us some very
important information regarding Mystery Babylon the Great.
Mystery Babylon the Great, as we will see in this vision, is a
key player in the events of the last days. In the next two chapters we will examine the characteristics which describe
"Mystery Babylon the Great," "the woman" and *"the prostitute."* Because of the key role she plays in the world and her
relationship to the fourth beast kingdom, it will be critical
that we identify her. Let's see how she is described:

One of the seven angels who had the seven bowls
came and said to me, "Come, I will show you the

punishment of the great prostitute, who sits on many waters. With her the kings of the earth committed adultery and the inhabitants of the earth were intoxicated with the wine of her adulteries." Then the angel carried me away in the Spirit into a desert. There I saw a woman sitting on a scarlet beast that was covered with blasphemous names and had seven heads and ten horns. The woman was dressed in purple and scarlet, and was glittering with gold, precious stones and pearls. She held a golden cup in her hand, filled with abominable things and the filth of her adulteries. This title was written on her forehead: MYSTERY BABYLON THE GREAT THE MOTHER OF PROSTITUTES AND OF THE ABOMINATIONS OF THE EARTH. I saw that the woman was drunk with the blood of the saints, the blood of those who bore testimony to Jesus. When I saw her, I was greatly astonished. Then the angel said to me: "Why are you astonished? I will explain to you the mystery of the woman and of the beast she rides, which has the seven heads and ten horns" (Revelation 17:1–7).

Here, we observe what appears to be a very wealthy and powerful city–state or nation identified as *"the prostitute,"* *"the woman"* and *"Mystery Babylon the Great."* In the first verse she is observed sitting on the many waters.

Then the angel said to me, "The waters you saw, where the prostitute sits, are peoples, multitudes, nations and languages. (Revelation 17:15).

From this we learn that Mystery Babylon in some way dominates the peoples, multitudes, nations and languages of the world. The expressions in this passage *"sits on"* and *"sitting on"* signify a position of dominance and influence. We are not told if this position of dominance is economic, military or political in nature. However, it is most likely all three.

The beast on which she is sitting is the fourth beast kingdom described in Daniel's prophecies. Daniel prophesied about this beast kingdom and how it came to have seven heads and ten horns. He also revealed that the Antichrist would rise to world dominance from this kingdom. Here is how it was explained to Daniel:

> *The ten horns are ten kings who will come from this kingdom. After them another king will arise, different from the earlier ones; he will subdue three kings* (Daniel 7:24).

Daniel was told the fourth beast kingdom would begin with ten kings or rulers. Then another king would arise from among them and overcome three of the original kings, leaving the fourth beast kingdom with seven heads. So, from that time, the fourth beast kingdom will have seven heads and ten horns. Therefore, the beast referred to in Revelation 17 is the fourth beast kingdom Daniel saw in his vision. Out of this fourth beast kingdom the Antichrist will rise to world dominance.

As we watch the picture develop in Revelation 17, we first see that *"Mystery Babylon the Great"* dominates the whole world. This superpower influences the world through its military, economic and political strength. However, *"Mystery Babylon the Great"* will ultimately be destroyed by what appears to be a conspiracy of the fourth beast kingdom. Let's see how John describes this:

> *The beast and the ten horns you saw will hate the prostitute. They will bring her to ruin and leave her*

naked; they will eat her flesh and burn her with fire.
For God has put it into their hearts to accomplish
his purpose by agreeing to give the beast their power
to rule, until God's words are fulfilled. The woman
you saw is the great city that rules over the kings of
the earth (Revelation 17:16–18).

John is saying that the Antichrist, and his kingdom with
its seven heads and ten horns, will hate Mystery Babylon.
This is an incredible prophecy of how the Antichrist and his
fourth beast kingdom will destroy Mystery Babylon and then
dominate the entire earth. The seven heads and ten horns will
be unified in their purpose and they will give their power to
the Antichrist. The Antichrist will use his power to destroy
Mystery Babylon the Great by fire. We will learn more of this
destruction by fire when we read Revelation 18.

The vision John had of the fourth beast kingdom
destroying Mystery Babylon the Great appears similar to
another prophecy of Daniel:

The king will do as he pleases. He will exalt and
magnify himself above every god and will say
unheard-of things against the God of gods. He will
be successful until the time of wrath is completed,
for what has been determined must take place. He
will show no regard for the gods of his fathers or
for the one desired by women, nor will he regard
any god, but will exalt himself above them all.
Instead of them, he will honor a god of fortresses;
a god unknown to his fathers he will honor with
gold and silver, with precious stones and costly
*gifts. **He will attack the mightiest fortresses** with*
the help of a foreign god and will greatly honor

those who acknowledge him. He will make them
rulers over many people and will distribute the land
at a price (Daniel 11:36–39).

When we compare John's and Daniel's prophecies, we come away with a picture of how this fourth kingdom develops and the Antichrist comes to power. Daniel writes that the king—the Antichrist—will successfully "attack the mightiest fortresses" with foreign help. Apparently, the Antichrist will also receive outside help in his conspiracy to destroy *"Mystery Babylon the Great."*

Christians and Bible students over the centuries have tried to determine the identity of *"Mystery Babylon the Great."* Let's first review the characteristics we find in chapter 17 before we move on to chapter 18.

Characteristics of "Mystery Babylon the Great":

1. She sits on peoples, multitudes, nations and languages.
2. The world is intoxicated with the wine of her adulteries.
3. She sits on the beast that has seven heads and ten horns.
4. She was drunk with the blood of the saints.
5. John was greatly astonished when he saw her.
6. The beast and the ten horns will hate her.
7. The beast will bring her to ruin and burn her with fire.
8. She is the great city that rules over the kings of the earth.

As with all biblical prophecy, each of these characteristics will be fulfilled by *"Mystery Babylon the Great."* If we put all of these characteristics together, this picture appears. *"Mystery Babylon the Great"* is a great city, probably part of a very powerful nation. She has power and influence over the peoples of the world and also the fourth beast kingdom of the Antichrist. The whole world desires what she has, which could be her way of life, her wealth and her power. In some way she is responsible for the death of people who would be considered the saints of God. She is probably a country who professes a faith in the true God, but has committed adultery by being unfaithful to the God she professes. The Antichrist and the fourth beast kingdom will hate her and destroy her with fire. With this in mind, let's read Revelation 18 to see what else we can learn about this last days superpower.

■ REVELATION 18—
MYSTERY BABYLON THE GREAT

In this chapter, John provides a rich and descriptive picture of *"Mystery Babylon the Great."* With the amount of detail provided, we should have little difficulty identifying *"Mystery Babylon the Great"* when she appears on the world scene. Once again, let's look at the characteristics attributed to her.

> *For all the nations have drunk the maddening wine of her adulteries. The kings of the earth committed adultery with her, and the merchants of the earth grew rich from her excessive luxuries....Give her as much torture and grief as the glory and luxury she gave herself* (Revelation 18:3,7).

Two of her main characteristics are her adulterous behavior and her excessive consumption. John actually lists many of the things she buys when describing her excessive consumption. Apparently, she consumes much of what the world produces because the "merchants of the earth grew rich from her excessive luxuries." *"Mystery Babylon the Great"* apparently is a nation on the sea or surrounded by the sea, because she receives what she consumes by sea, for we are told that "every sea captain...who earn their living from the sea," will weep and mourn when "*Mystery Babylon is destroyed.*"

Once again, the references to "*her adulteries*" may indicate that she is a country that proclaims a faith in the true God, but has not remained faithful. In Scripture, God referred to Israel's unfaithfulness in terms of adultery when she, who knew the one true God, abandoned Him for false gods and other forms of idolatry. Let's observe how God referred to Israel in this prophecy from Jeremiah: "*I gave faithless Israel her certificate of divorce and sent her away because of all her adulteries*" (Jeremiah 3:8).

Therefore, "*Mystery Babylon the Great*" is a rich superpower that professes a faith in the true God, but is really full of unbelief and disobedience. Again, John reveals that the final outcome of this wealthy superpower is destruction by fire in one day and one hour. Her destruction is both swift and complete.

> *Therefore in one day her plagues will overtake her: death, mourning and famine. She will be consumed by fire, for mighty is the Lord God who judges her. ...In one hour your doom has come! ...When they see the smoke of her burning, they will exclaim, 'Was there ever a city like this great city?'* (Revelation 18:8,10 and 18).

The destruction of "*Mystery Babylon the Great*" will apparently pave the way for the Antichrist and his fourth beast kingdom to rise to world dominance. "*Mystery Babylon the Great,*" who had dominated the world and the fourth beast kingdom, will be defeated never to rise again. When "*Mystery Babylon the Great*" is out of the way, the fourth beast kingdom and the Antichrist will be elevated to the position of superpower and world dominance—a position they will maintain until the end.

When the Antichrist and his kingdom destroy "*Mystery Babylon the Great*," the world will certainly say, "*Who is like the beast? Who can make war against him?*" (Revelation 13:4).

■ REVELATION 19—
THE COMING OF THE LORD

Once again, the vision changes and we see what appears to be the final preparations before the coming of the Lord.

> *Then I heard what sounded like a great multitude, like the roar of rushing waters and like loud peals of thunder, shouting: Hallelujah! For our Lord God Almighty reigns. Let us rejoice and be glad and give him glory! For the wedding of the Lamb has come, and his bride has made herself ready* (Revelation 19:6,7).

This is the second time the "*great multitude*" is mentioned in connection with the preparations being made for the Lord's return, here and in Revelation 7:9. The "*great multitude*" is all the saints who have died in Christ. They are given fine linen, bright and clean, to wear as they are readied for the "*harvest*" which will occur at the return of Christ. Now the vision shifts to Christ.

> *I saw heaven standing open and there before me was a white horse, whose rider is called Faithful and True. With justice he judges and makes war* (Revelation 19:11).

Christ is seen in heaven just before He returns to gather his

Bride in preparation for the wedding supper on Mount Zion in Jerusalem (Isaiah 25:6–8).

In the subsequent verses of Revelation 19, the Antichrist, the kings of the earth and their armies are gathered together for the great and final battle of Armageddon. The Antichrist and the False Prophet are captured and thrown into the lake of fire, and then Christ slaughters their armies, leaving them for the birds of the air.

■ REVELATION 20

After the capture of the two beasts and the defeat of their armies, Satan will be bound and thrown into the Abyss for *"a thousand years."* Sealed in the Abyss, he will be unable to deceive the nations for the thousand-year reign of Christ on earth. Here is how Isaiah saw Satan's defeat:

> *All your pomp has been brought down to the grave, along with the noise of your harps; maggots are spread out beneath you and worms cover you. How you have fallen from heaven, O morning star, son of the dawn! You have been cast down to the earth, you who once laid low the nations! You said in your heart, "I will ascend to heaven; I will raise my throne above the stars of God; I will sit enthroned on the mount of assembly, on the utmost heights of the sacred mountain. I will ascend above the tops of the clouds; I will make myself like the Most High." But you are brought down to the grave, to the depths of the pit (Isaiah 14:11–15).*

John then sees another vision and he describes the *"first resurrection,"* which is the resurrection of the righteous, of those who will reign with Christ for *"a thousand years."*

*I saw thrones on which were seated those who had been given authority to judge. And I saw the souls of those who had been beheaded because of their testimony for Jesus and because of the word of God. They had not worshiped the beast or his image and had not received his mark on their foreheads or their hands. **They came to life and reigned with Christ a thousand years.** (The rest of the dead did not come to life until the thousand years were ended.) **This is the first resurrection.** Blessed and holy are those who have part in the first resurrection. The second death has no power over them, but they will be priests of God and of Christ and will reign with him for a thousand years* (Revelation 20:4–6).

This passage provides important information to our study of the last days and the return of Christ. We are now told that the earthly reign of Christ, which has been prophesied throughout Scripture, will last "*a thousand years.*" We are also told that the saints who take part in the "*first resurrection*" are martyred during the Great Tribulation. We know they are killed after the Antichrist is revealed, because the beast, his image and his mark are all present. Therefore, the "*first resurrection*" takes place after the Great Tribulation.

In this passage, John says the martyred saints of the Great Tribulation are part of the "*first resurrection.*" However, these martyred saints are not the only saints who are part of the "*first resurrection,*" because we have already seen in Scripture that this is the time when all the saints will be resurrected. Recall the way Paul describes the resurrection:

*For since death came through a man, **the resurrection** of the dead comes also through a man. For as* *in Adam all die, so in Christ all will be made alive. But each in his own turn: **Christ, the first fruits; then, when he comes, those who belong to him** (1 Corinthians 15:21–23).*

John also tells us that the rest of the dead, those who have died and not taken part in the *"first resurrection,"* will be raised after *"a thousand years."* Apparently, the rest of the dead are raised at a second resurrection. John sees that the rest of the dead are raised and judged at the *"great white throne."*

Then I saw a great white throne and him who was seated on it. Earth and sky fled from his presence, and there was no place for them. And I saw the dead, great and small, standing before the throne, and books were opened. Another book was opened, which is the book of life. The dead were judged according to what they had done as recorded in the books. The sea gave up the dead that were in it, and death and Hades gave up the dead that were in them, and each person was judged according to what he had done. Then death and Hades were thrown into the lake of fire. The lake of fire is the second death. If anyone's name was not found written in the book of life, he was thrown into the lake of fire (Revelation 20:11–15).

It appears that the second resurrection includes all those who have died apart from Christ since the beginning of creation. This would include everyone who name is not found written in the book of life. They will be judged and thrown into the lake of fire with Satan, the Antichrist and the False Prophet, where they will be tormented forever and ever.

What happens after the thousand-year reign of Christ

has not been described extensively in Scripture. Therefore, it is difficult to say with certainty what exactly will happen. However, Paul provides insight when he tells us, in 1 Corinthians 15, that Christ will reign until He has accomplished everything and then God will become the "*all in all*." This is how Paul describes what will happen following the thousand years of Christ's reign on earth.

> *For he must reign until he has put all his enemies under his feet. The last enemy to be destroyed is death. For he 'has put everything under his feet.' Now when it says that 'everything' has been put under him, it is clear that this does not include God himself, who put everything under Christ. When he has done this, then the Son himself will be made subject to him who put everything under him, so that God may be all in all* (1 Corinthians 15:25–28).

■ REVELATION 21—
NEW HEAVEN AND NEW EARTH

Once again, John tells of another vision that does not follow in chronological order. Instead of taking place after the Millennium, this vision is of the "*first resurrection*" when Christ comes down to the earth with His bride. There are several indications in the text that place this scene at the coming of Christ:

> *Then I saw a new heaven and a new earth, for the first heaven and the first earth had passed away, and there was no longer any sea. I saw the Holy City, the new Jerusalem, coming down out of heaven from God, prepared as a* **bride** *beautifully dressed for her husband. And I heard a loud voice from the throne saying,* "**Now the dwelling of God is with men,** *and he will*

*live with them. They will be his people, and **God himself will be with them** and be their God. **He will wipe every tear** from their eyes. **There will be no more death** or mourning or crying or pain, for the **old order of things has passed away**"* (Revelation 21:1–4).

First, we know that at the return of Christ, He will gather His bride and meet her in the air as He comes to earth to establish the Kingdom on earth. Therefore, when we see the *"Bride"* of Christ coming down, we know this takes place at Christ's coming in glory.

Second, John tells us that at this time, the *"dwelling of God is with man"* and He *"will be with them."* Again, this also happens when Jesus returns, because when we are gathered to Him, as described in 1 Thessalonians 4, it is written, *"we will be with him forever."*

Third, John tells us *"He will wipe away every tear,"* and *"There will be no more death,"* and *"the old order of things has passed away."* Each of these things will have already taken place at the *"first resurrection."* Therefore, everything we see happening in this vision will take place at the time of Christ's return, not after the 1,000 years.

Finally, as John describes the New Jerusalem coming down as the Bride of Christ from heaven, the symbolism portrays the picture of the Bride of Christ coming down as she does at Christ's coming. Therefore, once again, we can see that this event will actually take place at the beginning of the thousand-year reign of Christ on earth, not after.

■ REVELATION 22—
WHEN THE LORD COMES

Continuing the same picture from Revelation 21, John now tells us how things will be when the Kingdom of God is established on the new earth:

> *Then the angel showed me the river of the water of life, as clear as crystal, flowing from the throne of God and of the Lamb down the middle of the great street of the city. On each side of the river stood the tree of life, bearing twelve crops of fruit, yielding its fruit every month. And the leaves of the tree are for the healing of the nations.* **No longer will there be any curse.** *The throne of God and of the Lamb will be in the city, and his servants will serve him.* **They will see his face,** *and his name will be on their foreheads. There will be no more night. They will not need the light of a lamp or the light of the sun, for the Lord God will give them light. And they will reign forever and ever* (Revelation 22:1–5).

"*No longer will there be any curse*" when the Lord restores everything at His return. Then John tells us that Christ's servants "*will see His face,*" which occurs when we meet Him in the air. Therefore, from the content of this entire vision, we plainly see a picture of the coming of Christ and the Bride of Christ at the beginning of His reign on earth.

Now that the vision of the last days is complete, Jesus begins to close the Revelation with assurance that His coming is soon:

> *Behold, I am coming soon! My reward is with me, and I will give to everyone according to what he has done. I am the Alpha and the Omega, the First and the Last, the Beginning and the End. Blessed are those who wash their robes, that they may have the right to the tree of life and may go through the gates into the city* (Revelation 22:12–14).

Note that Jesus calls Himself *"the First and the Last."* This is a title the Lord God almighty uses for Himself: *"This is what the* LORD *says—Israel's King and Redeemer, the* LORD *Almighty: 'I am the first and I am the last; apart from me there is no God'"* (Isaiah 44:6).

Once again, Jesus clearly claims to be God—just as He did throughout His earthly ministry. As the Word of God declares, Jesus the Christ is one with the Father and God Almighty. He created all things, and He will restore and establish all things just as He has declared in His Word. God has revealed His plan, His purpose and His character in His Word, and He warns us in these closing words that we are not to add to what He has written; nor are we to take away from what He has written. Read for yourself the most severe warning in Scripture, against incorrectly handling the Word of Truth:

> *I warn everyone who hears the words of the prophecy of this book:* **If anyone adds anything to them, God will add to him the plagues described in this book. And if anyone takes words away from this book of prophecy, God will take away from him his share in the tree of life** *and in the holy city, which are described in this book* (Revelation 22:18,19).

The biblical warning instructing us not to add or take away from the Word of God was first written in the Old Testament (Deuteronomy 4:2). But in no place in Scripture is this warning stronger than it is here, concerning Christ's return. Therefore, everyone who preaches and teaches the Word of God would be wise to take note of the consequences for going beyond what is written.

Yes, I am coming soon (Revelation 22:20).

CHAPTER NINE

The Last Days' Timeline

"But mark this: There will be terrible times in the last days" (2 Timothy 3:1).

Almost 2,000 years ago the Son of God came to earth. At His coming, He literally fulfilled hundreds of Old Testament prophecies and revealed Himself to be the Anointed One and only Son of God. He taught and prophesied about the coming Kingdom and claimed that He was God. He was called Jesus of Nazareth; He was the long awaited Messiah, the King of the Jews, as prophesied in Daniel 9:25 over 600 years earlier.

Jesus entered Jerusalem and offered Himself as King of the Jews, in the year and on the exact day that Daniel foretold. Daniel prophesied that the Messiah the King would make a covenant by sacrifice, which Jesus did when He gave His life for the sin of the world. Daniel also prophesied that Jerusalem and the temple would be destroyed which it was in A.D. 70.

Below is a brief timeline of Daniel's "Seventy Weeks" prophecy.

Daniel's Seventy Weeks = 490 years

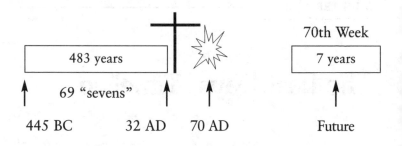

To date, sixty-nine "sevens" of Daniel's prophecy have been completely fulfilled, which leaves just one seven-year period unfulfilled. This remaining seven-year period is called Daniel's seventieth week.

At the end of Jesus' First Advent, He ascended into heaven from the Mount of Olives. But before He left, he instructed the Church to make disciples, to baptize them and teach them to obey everything He had commanded until His return. During Christ's First Advent, He prophesied about the signs and the circumstances that would characterize His return at the end of the age.

Last Days Timeline

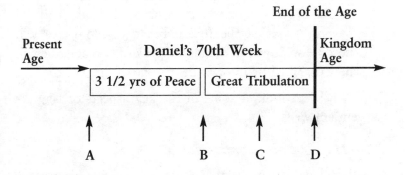

■ PRESENT AGE

The Present Age is the time from Adam to the end of the age. Since Christ's crucifixion, at least two biblical prophecies have been fulfilled. First, the destruction of Jerusalem and Herod's Temple (Daniel 19:26, Matthew 24:2, Mark 13:2, Luke 19:44, and Luke 21:6). Second, the restoration of Israel as a nation on May 14, 1948 (Ezekiel 39:27 and Micah 5:3).

There are even now a number of biblical prophecies remaining which must be fulfilled before we reach Daniel's seventieth week. Three of these are:

1. The rise of a world superpower, known as Mystery Babylon the Great, as prophesied in Revelation 17 and 18. This wealthy superpower will exercise authority and influence over the whole world until it is destroyed by a conspiracy headed by the Antichrist.
2. The rise to power of the Fourth Beast Kingdom as prophesied in Daniel 7:23–25 and Revelation 17:9–16. This kingdom will dominate the whole world by force once it has destroyed Mystery Babylon the Great.

3. The rise of the beast known as the Antichrist as prophesied in Daniel 7:23–25 and Revelation 13:1–8. This powerful and extremely successful world leader will rise to power out of the fourth beast kingdom. He will become so powerful that at the peak of his career he will be worshiped by most of the people of the world.

Now, let's look at some of the key aspects of Daniel's seventieth week.

A—The covenant confirmed

Israel will continue to be a center of trouble for the world (Zechariah 12:2) until the Antichrist confirms a covenant of peace with Israel, as prophesied in Daniel 9:27 and Isaiah 28:15–18. *"He will confirm a covenant with many for one 'seven'"* (Daniel 9:27);

> *You boast, "We have entered into a covenant with death, with the grave we have made an agreement. When an overwhelming scourge sweeps by, it cannot touch us, for we have made a lie our refuge and falsehood our hiding place"* (Isaiah 28:15).

B—The abomination that causes desolation

The covenant made with the Antichrist will not last. *"In the middle of the 'seven' he will put an end to sacrifice and offering. And on a wing of the temple he will set up an abomination that causes desolation"* (Daniel 9:27); *"While people are saying, "Peace and safety," destruction will come on them suddenly, as labor pains on a pregnant woman, and they will not escape"* (1 Thessalonians 5:3); *"Your covenant with death will be annulled; your agreement with the grave will not stand. When the overwhelming scourge sweeps by, you will be beaten down by it"* (Isaiah 28:18).

After three and a half years of peace, the Antichrist will set himself up as God in the temple of God. By that time, a new Jewish temple will have been built on the temple mount in Jerusalem. Today, even though Israel has possession of the temple mount, they are unable to rebuild the temple because of the presence of the Dome of the Rock and the Al Aksa Mosque. The temple mount is also a Muslim holy site (Haram al-Sharif), and because of the religious strife between the Jews and Muslims, it is currently impossible to rebuild the temple. The Bible strongly indicates, however, that there will be a Jewish temple by the time of the *abomination that causes desolation.*

There is no indication in Scripture regarding when the temple will be reconstructed. It may be rebuilt during the Present Age or at the latest during the first half of Daniel's seventieth week. However, we know that the temple will be rebuilt.

The *abomination that causes desolation* is a very significant event. Jesus gave it as the first of the specific signs of His return and the end of the age. This event has been prophesied about in Scripture from Isaiah to Revelation. It takes place in the middle of Daniel's seventieth week, point "B" on the time line.

C—The Great Tribulation

When the Antichrist declares that he is God in the temple of God, he will also begin the time of unprecedented persecution known as the Great Tribulation. This three and a half year time span is referred to as:

1. *A time, times and half a time*—Daniel 7:25, 12:7 and Revelation 12:14
2. *In the middle of the 'seven'*—Daniel 9:27

3. *42 months*—Revelation 11:2
4. *1,260 days*—Revelation 11:3 and 12:6

This period of tribulation and testing will also be a time of incredible supernatural activity on the earth and in the lives of mankind. The following list includes some of the signs and events that will take place during the Great Tribulation, "C" on the time line.

Signs prophesied to occur during the Great Tribulation:

(These signs are not necessarily in chronological order.)

1. The "rebellion" or "falling away" from the faith (2 Thessalonians 2:3, Matthew 24:9–11, Daniel 8:11,12).
2. The Antichrist will persecute and kill the people of God (Revelation 12:13–17; 13:5–7, Daniel 8:11,12).
3. The Jewish remnant will flee into the wilderness for three and a half years (Revelation 12:14).
4. Angels will proclaim the gospel, announce the fall of "Mystery Babylon the Great" and warn the world not to worship the beast or take his mark (Revelation 14:6–11 and Matthew 24:14).
5. The two witnesses will prophesy for 1,260 days (Revelation 11:3–13).
6. A second beast, called the False Prophet, will perform great signs to deceive the world and cause everyone to worship the Antichrist and receive his mark or be killed (Revelation 13:11-18).
7. The sun, moon and stars will be darkened before the Day of the Lord (Joel 2:31, Matthew 24:29, Isaiah 13:10 and Acts 2:20).

D—End of the age

The disciples asked Jesus *"what will be the sign of your*

coming and the end of the age?" Their question reflects their understanding that His return would be at the end of the age. Jesus had taught them that the *harvest,* which is the resurrection of believers, would come at the end of the age. They also wanted to know what signs would signal His return. Jesus gave them several signs and warned them to *"watch"* and *"stay alert"* because of the great deception that would come in the last days. Here is what the Lord has revealed will occur—on the Day of the Lord—at the end of the age.

■ PROPHESIES TO BE FULFILLED ON THE DAY OF THE LORD:

(These are not necessarily in chronological order.)

1. The Son of Man will come down from heaven and will appear in the clouds of the sky with His holy angels (Matthew 24:30).

2. The seventh and last trumpet will sound (Matthew 24:31, 1Corinthians 15:52, 1 Thessalonians 4:16 and Revelations 11:15).

3. The elect of God will be gathered at the resurrection (Psalm 50:4,5, Daniel 12:1, Matthew 24:31, 1 Corinthians 15:51 and 1 Thessalonians 4:15–17).

4. The Lord Jesus Christ will judge His people (Psalm 50:4,5, Revelation 11:18).

5. The Lord will stand on the Mount of Olives (Zechariah 14:4).

6. The Lord will prepare a wedding feast on Mount Zion (Isaiah 25:6–8).

7. The kingdom of this world will become the Kingdom of our Lord (Revelation 11:15; 20:4–6).

8. The wrath of God will be poured out on the unbelieving and disobedient world (Revelation 19:17–19; 16:16).

■ The Kingdom Age

The Day of the Lord also ushers in the Kingdom Age which is the thousand-year reign of Christ on the earth. On the Day of the Lord, Christ will renew everything and restore Israel. Jesus will reign from the throne of David in Jerusalem, as it is written:

> *Of the increase of his government and peace there will be no end. He will reign on David's throne and over his kingdom, establishing and upholding it with justice and righteousness from that time on and forever* (Isaiah 9:7).

> *Then the sovereignty, power and greatness of the kingdoms under the whole heaven will be handed over to the saints, the people of the Most High* (Daniel 7:27).

After the 1,000 years, He will turn everything over to the Father so that God will be *"**all in all**."*

CHAPTER TEN

You Have Heard It Said

You have heard that it was said, 'Love your neighbor and hate your enemy. But I tell you: Love your enemies and pray for those who persecute you (Matthew 5:43,44).

A method Jesus used in His teaching was to contrast a popular belief with His Word. Jesus would begin by saying, *"You have heard that it was said,"* and He would state a belief which the people held to be true. He would then instruct them by saying, *"But I tell you."*

It appears He used this method for two reasons—first, to show the people a deeper meaning of an existing teaching; second, to correct a misinterpretation by revealing that they could not always trust what they heard. In each case, He would provide the correct teaching by saying, *"But I tell you."* What Jesus was saying to the crowds, then, is the same thing He is saying to us today—be careful not to believe everything you hear, and to test everything by the Word of God. During Jesus' time on earth the people received the truth directly from the Word made flesh, Jesus

Christ. Today, we, too, receive the truth from the Word, as it is written in Scripture.

In the old adventure novels, pirates and seafarers were famous for saying, "I don't believe anything I hear and only half of what I see, because things are not as they appear." The Bible also warns us to test everything, because many false teachers will appear and deceive many. Today, more than ever, Christians need to be like the Bereans and rely on Scripture to determine the truth. The Scripture reveals that man is prone to deception, often being carried away by false doctrine and quick to run after teachings that sound good. The Lord has provided the truth in His Word to protect us from false doctrine and deception. The Word needs to be the final authority and the touchstone of truth for our lives or we will certainly be led astray. Therefore, listen intently but always examine Scripture to determine what is true.

Once again, Jesus would say, *"You have heard that it was said,"* and then He would say, *"But I tell you."* To demonstrate how this method of teaching works we will now look at some of the things we have heard about the last days, then we will examine the Scriptures to see what is true.

1. *You have heard it said that the Church will be raptured before the Tribulation begins, but the Bible says:*

   Immediately after the [tribulation] *distress of those days 'the sun will be darkened, and the moon will not give its light; the stars will fall from the sky, and the heavenly bodies will be shaken.' At that time the sign of the Son of Man will appear in the sky, and all the nations of the earth will mourn. They will see the Son of Man coming on the clouds of the sky, with power and great glory. And he will send his angels with a loud trumpet call, and they will gather his elect from the four winds, from one end of the heavens to the other* (Matthew 24:29–31).

Jesus clearly states that He will come and gather His elect after the Great Tribulation.

2. **You have heard it said that the Church will be raptured from the earth before the Antichrist is revealed, but the Bible says:**

   Concerning the coming of our Lord Jesus Christ and our being gathered to him, we ask you, brothers, not to become easily unsettled or alarmed by some prophecy, report or letter supposed to have come from us, saying that the Day of the Lord has already come. Don't let anyone deceive you in any way, for that day will not come until the rebellion occurs and the man of lawlessness is revealed, the man doomed to destruction (2 Thessalonians 2:1–3).

   Paul clearly states that the Antichrist will be revealed first and then the Lord will come and gather the Church to himself.

3. **You have heard it said that the First Resurrection will take place before the Great Tribulation, but the Bible says:**

   I saw the souls of those who had been beheaded because of their testimony for Jesus and because of the word of God. They had not worshiped the beast or his image and had not received his mark on their foreheads or their hands. They came to life and reigned with Christ a thousand years. (The rest of the dead did not come to life until the thousand

years were ended.) This is the first resurrection.
Blessed and holy are those who have part in the first
resurrection (Revelation 20:4–6).

John clearly states that the *"first resurrection"* will include the saints who did not worship the beast or take his mark. Since, the Antichrist and his mark will occur during the Great Tribulation; the *"first resurrection"* must be after the Great Tribulation.

4. **You have heard it said, that Jesus could come at any moment to rapture the Church, and that nothing has to happesn before His coming, but the Bible says:**

[Jesus said,] *"…when you see all these things, you know that it is near, right at the door"* (Matthew 24:33).

Jesus told us several things that we would see, as signs, before His coming and he also said, *"Therefore, keep watch"* (Matthew 24:42).

Paul also told us that we will see the Day of the Lord approaching and it will not surprise us because we will recognize the signs of its approaching. *"But you, brothers, are not in darkness so that this day should surprise you like a thief* (1 Thessalonians 5:5).

God said in Hebrews that we would see the day approaching, which would not be possible if there was nothing to look for. *"Let us not give up meeting together, as some are in the habit of doing, but let us encourage one another—and all the more as you see the Day approaching"* (Hebrews 10:25).

Therefore, the Scripture states that there will be signs and events that will take place before the Lord's return. It is also written that the return of Christ on the Day of the

Lord will not surprise the believers, because they will see the day approaching.

5. You have heard it said that Jesus will come first to secretly Rapture His Church, but the Bible says:

"This same Jesus, who has been taken from you into heaven, will come back in the same way you have seen him go into heaven" (Acts 1:11); "For as lightning that comes from the east is visible even in the west, so will be the coming of the Son of Man" (Matthew 24:27).

The return of Christ is always described, in Scripture, as highly visible and there is not a single verse in the Word of God which states in any way that the return of Christ will be either silent or secret.

6. You have heard it said that Jesus will rapture his Church and then take us back to heaven, but the Bible says:

On that day his feet will stand on the Mount of Olives, east of Jerusalem, ... the Lord will come, and all the holy ones with Him (Zechariah 14:4,5).

On this mountain the LORD Almighty will prepare a feast of rich food for all peoples, a banquet of aged wine— the best of meats and the finest of wines. On this mountain he will destroy the shroud that enfolds all peoples, the sheet that covers all nations; he will swallow up death forever. The Sovereign LORD will wipe away the tears from all faces; he will remove the disgrace of his people from all the earth. The LORD has spoken. In that day they will say, "Surely this is our God; we trusted in him, and he saved us (Isaiah 25:6–9).

The Lord clearly states through His prophets that when He returns on the Day of the Lord, He will come to earth and prepare the wedding feast for His Bride, the Body of Christ.

7. *You have heard it said that the Church is not present in Revelation after chapter three, but the Bible says:*

The dragon was enraged at the woman and went off to make war against the rest of her offspring—those who obey God's commandments and hold to the testimony of Jesus (Revelation 12:17).

This calls for patient endurance and faithfulness on the part of the saints (Revelation 13:10).

Jesus clearly identifies His followers—the saints—those who hold to the testimony of Jesus—His servants and brothers—as going through the period of persecution known as the Great Tribulation. To say that the Church is not present just because the word *church* is not used is misleading and deceptive.

8. *You have heard it said that the Gospel of Matthew is not for the Church because it is a Jewish gospel, but the Bible says:*

And I tell you that you are Peter, and on this rock I will build my church, and the gates of Hades will not overcome it. I will give you the keys of the Kingdom of heaven; whatever you bind on earth will be bound in heaven, and whatever you loose on earth will be loosed in heaven (Matthew 16:18,19).

But if he will not listen, take one or two others along, so that 'every matter may be established by the testimony of two or three witnesses.' If he refuses to listen to them, tell it to the church; and if he refuses to listen even to the church, treat him as you would a pagan or a tax collector (Matthew 18:16,17).

Then he took the cup, gave thanks and offered it to them, saying, "Drink from it, all of you. This is my blood of the covenant, which is poured out for many for the forgiveness of sins. I tell you, I will not drink of this fruit of the vine from now on until that day when I drink it anew with you in my Father's Kingdom" (Matthew 26:27–29).

Then Jesus came to them and said, "All authority in heaven and on earth has been given to me. Therefore go and make disciples of all nations, baptizing them in the name of the Father and of the Son and of the Holy Spirit, and teaching them to obey everything I have commanded you. And surely I am with you always, to the very end of the age" (Matthew 28:18–20).

To say that any part of the Gospel of Matthew is not for the Church is to ignore that Matthew has more to say about the Church than any of the other Gospels. In fact, since Matthew is the only Gospel to mention the Church by name, it could be called the Church Gospel. However, since Matthew also contains a strong Jewish perspective, it would be best to call Matthew the Believers' Gospel, because that is certainly who it is written for.

■ BE CAREFUL THAT NO ONE DECEIVES YOU.

Today we are being told that the Bible says many things which it doesn't say and a great deal of new theology is being written and preached. One new theology teaches that Jesus is going to return for His Church before the Antichrist appears and before the Great Tribulation begins. This new theology also teaches that Jesus will return from heaven, gather up His Church and then return to heaven for the Judgment Seat of Christ and the Wedding Supper of the Lamb. Further, this new theology teaches that while the Church is in heaven, the Antichrist will be reigning supreme on earth, persecuting the Jewish people and the left-behind followers of Christ. This new theology also says that, following this time of persecution, Jesus will return a second time with His Church. This Coming will be to punish the unbelieving world, defeat the Antichrist and set up the Kingdom of God on earth. This new theology, which includes a Pre-Tribulation Rapture, has emerged within the last 180 years.

The Bible, however, makes absolutely no statement which supports a Pre-Tribulation Rapture. This new theology is based on **allegories** and its foundation is built on sinking sand. This allegorical method of interpretation contradicts Scripture on two fronts. **First,** it does not follow the biblical rules for "*correctly handling the Word of Truth,*" (see chapter one of this book). **Second,** it completely changes the way the Bible has been understood through the centuries. All biblical prophecy, which has been fulfilled, has always been fulfilled at face value, in its normal, literal sense. Also, whenever an individual in Scripture is referencing biblical prophecy, they always interpret Scripture at face value, in its normal, literal sense. For example, when Daniel was reading from the prophet Jeremiah, he interpreted the prophecy to mean just what it said, not something else.

In the first year of his reign, I, Daniel, understood from the Scriptures, according to the word of the

LORD *given to Jeremiah the prophet, that the desolation of Jerusalem would last seventy years* (Daniel 9:2).

Up until the last 180 years, the Church has taught and preached that the Antichrist will come and persecute the Church during the Great Tribulation and then Christ will return at the end of the age, resurrect the dead and rescue those who are left alive at that time.

As you will see from the following quotes, representative of the first nineteen centuries of church writings, a Post-Tribulation view was the common view. They believed the clear teachings of Scripture, that the Church would face the Antichrist and go through the Great Tribulation before Christ returned. Read these examples and see for yourself.

Didache (A.D. 100)—"then shall appear the world-deceiver as Son of God, and shall do signs and wonders, and the earth shall be delivered into his hands... but they that endure in their faith shall be saved from under the curse itself. And then shall appear the signs of the truth; first, the sign of an out-spreading in heaven; then the sign of the sound of the trumpet; and the third, the resurrection of the dead; yet not of all, but as it is said: The Lord shall come and all His saints with Him. Then shall the world see the Lord coming upon the clouds of heaven." (Didache—Chapter 16)[1]

Justin Martyr (A.D. 100–168)—"Two Advents of Christ have been announced: the one, in which He is set forth as suffering, inglorious, dishonored, and crucified; but the other, in which He shall come from heaven with glory, when the man of apostasy, who speaks strange things against the Most High, shall venture to do unlawful deeds on the earth against us the Christians, (First Apology of Justine, Chapter 110)[2]

Tertullian (A.D. 150–220)—that the beast Antichrist, with his false prophet may wage war on the Church of God; (On the Resurrection of the Flesh, 25)[3]

Irenaeus (A.D. 140–202)—and put the church to flight. After that they shall be destroyed by the Coming of our Lord." (Against Heresies V, XXVI, 1)[4]

Cyprian (A.D. 200–258)—"[T]he Lord hath foretold that these things would come. With the exhortation of His forseeing word, instructing, and teaching, and preparing, and strengthening the people of His Church for all endurance of things to come. He previously warned us that the adversary would increase more and more in the last times." (Treatise 7) "For you ought to know and to believe, and hold it for certain, that the day of affliction has begun to hang over our heads, and the end of the world and the time of Antichrist to draw near, so that we must all stand prepared for the battle ... The time cometh, that whosoever killeth you will think that he doeth God service..." Nor let any one wonder that we are harassed with increasing afflictions, when the Lord before predicted that these things would happen in the last times (Epistles of Cyprian, LV, 1,2). *Nor let any one of you, beloved brethren, be so terrified by the fear of future persecution, or the coming of the threatening Antichrist, as not to be found armed for*

all things by the evangelical exhortations and pre-
cepts, and by the heavenly warnings. Antichrist is
coming... but immediately the Lord follows to
avenge our sufferings and our wounds (Epistles of
Cyprian, LIII, p.722).[5]

Victorinus (A.D. **269–271**)—"He shall cause also that
a golden image of Antichrist shall be placed in the
temple at Jerusalem, and that the apostate angel
should enter, and thence utter voices and oracles...
The Lord, admonishing *His churches concerning the*
last times and their dangers, ... three years and six
months, in which with all his power the devil will
avenge himself under Antichrist against the Church."
(Commentary on the Apocalypse, 20:1–3).[6]

Hippolytus (A.D. **160–240**)—" ...the one thousand
two hundred and three score days (the half of the
week) during which the tyrant is to reign and persecute the Church ..." (Treatise on Christ and
Antichrist, 61).[7]

Augustine (A.D. **354–430**)—"...the kingdom of
Antichrist shall fiercely, though for a short time,
assail the Church..." (The City of God, XX, 23).[8]

Roger Bacon (A.D. **1214–1274**)—" ...future perils
[for the Church] in the times of Antichrist..." (Opus
Majus II, p. 634).[9]

Martin Luther (A.D. **1483–1546**)—"[The Book of
Revelation] is intended as a revelation of things that
are to happen in the future, and especially of tribu-
lations and disasters for the Church...." (Works of
Martin Luther, VI, p. 481).[10]

John Knox (A.D. 1515–1572)—"the great love of God towards his Church, whom he pleased to forewarne of dangers to come... to wit, The man of sin, The Antichrist..." (The Historie of the Reformation etc., 1, p. 76).[11]

Roger Williams (A.D. 1603–1683)—"Antichrist... hath his prisons, to keep Christ Jesus and his members fast " (The Bloody Tenent etc., p. 153).[12]

Charles Hodge (A.D. 1797–1878)—"...the fate of his Church here on earth... is the burden of the Apocalypse" (Systematic Theology, III, p. 827).[14]

Carl F. Keil (A.D. 1807–1888)—"...the persecution of the last enemy Antichrist against the Church of the Lord ... (Biblical Commentary, YXMV, p. 503).[15]

Beginning in about 1832, a new teaching and theology began to creep into the churches. One of the first to teach this view was John Nelson Darby, the father of modern Dispensationalism. His theology was later picked up by C.I. Scofield and popularized in *The Scofield Study Bible*. Several evangelical schools adopted the Dispensational Theology and began to teach it and incorporate it into their doctrinal positions. Many wrote and taught versions of Dispensationalism, but the most popular idea promoted by this theology was a Pre-Tribulation Rapture of the Church. This idea is very appealing, because it teaches that the Church will not have to face the tribulation of the last seven-year period prophesied in Daniel 9:27. Many authors and teachers have become incredibly popular promoting the idea of a Pre-Tribulation escape for the Church, and have been able to sell millions of books. Today, in Christian bookstores, the most popular end-times books, whether theological or fictional, promote this new teaching of a Pre-Tribulation Rapture. There have even been feature-length motion pictures released promoting this new doctrine.

The original and true teaching of Scripture is now maintained by a relatively small remnant of believers. They continue to hold to the clear statements of the Word of God on the topic of the return of Christ at the end of the age. True biblical teaching states that the resurrection of all believers will take place at the end of the reign of the Antichrist, when Jesus returns to establish the Kingdom on the Day of the Lord.

I will close with these words of wisdom and warning from Isaiah: *"To the law and to the testimony! If they do not speak according to this word, they have no light of dawn"* (Isaiah 8:20).

May the Lord Jesus Christ bless and guide you as you seek to know and obey Him.

He who testifies to these things says, 'Yes, I am coming soon.' Amen. Come, Lord Jesus. The grace of the Lord Jesus be with God's people. Amen (Revelation 22:20,21).

BIBLIOGRAPHY

Books from my library which I have read or consulted during this study. However, the only book I truly recommend you read and study is the Holy Bible.

The Holy Bible.

Allis, Oswald. *The Unity of Isaiah—A Study in Prophecy* 1980.

—————. *Prophecy And The Church*, 1945.

Anderson, Sir Robert, *Daniel In The Critics Den.*

—————. *The Coming Prince*, 1957.

Andrews, Samuel J., *Christianity—AntiChristianity—Final Conflict*, 1889.

Archer, Gleason, *Three Views On The Rapture*, 1996.

Arnold, William III, *The Post-Tribulation Rapture*, 1999.

Bachicha, Martin, *The Kingdom Of The Bride*, 1997.

Bahnsen and Gentry, *House Divided—The Break-up of Dispensational Theology*, 1997.

Bass, Clarence B. *Backgrounds to Dispensationalism*, 1960.

Beasley-Murray, G. *Jesus And The Last Days—Olivet Discourse*, 1993.

Beckwith, George. *God's Prophetic Plan Through The Ages*,

1947.

Beckwith, Isbon. *The Apocalypse of John*, 1919.

Bennett, Travis. *Posttribulational Questions for Pretribulational Brethren.*

Berkhof, L. *The Kingdom Of God*, 1951.

Bonar, Andrew *Development of Antichrist*, 1853.

Biederwolf, William E, *The Prophecy Handbook*, 1924.

———————. *The Second Coming Bible*, 1977.

Blackstone, William E. *Jesus Is Coming*, 1908.

Bloomfield, Arthur. *Armageddon, Before The Last Battle*, 1971.

Bloomfield, Arthur. *The End Of The Days*, 1961.

Bruce, F. F. *Commentary—1 & 2 Thessalonians*, 1982.

Bussard, Dave. *Who Will Be Left Behind and When?* 2002.

Buxton, Clyne. *End Times*, 1997.

Calvin, John. *Commentaries On The Prophet Daniel*, 1617.

Carroll, B. H. *The Book of Revelation*, 1913.

Charles, R. H. *The Revelation of John*, 1920.

———————. *Eschatology*, 1963.

Chilton, David. *The Days Of Vengeance*, 1987.

Cho, David Y. *The Apocalyptic Prophecy*, 1990.

Cox, William E. *Biblical Studies In Final Things*, 1966.

Cronk, Gerald. *Now about that Rapture... When?* 1997.

Culver, Robert Duncan. *The Histories And Prophecies of Daniel*, 1980.

Dake, Finis Jennings. *The Rapture And The Second Coming of Christ.*

Dana, H. E. *The Epistles and Apocalypse of John*, 1937.

Douty, Norman F. *The Great Tribulation Debate*, 1976.

Edersheim, Alfred.. *The Temple Its Ministry and Services*, 1958.

Efird, James M. *End Times, Rapture, Antichrist, Millennium*, 1946.

Eller, Vernard. *The Most Revealing Book Of The Bible*, 1974.

English, Schuyler. *Re-Thinking the Rapture*, 1954.

Erdman, Charles R. *The Revelation of John*, 1929.

——————. *The Return of Christ*, 1922.

Evans, Tony. *Bible Prophecies Through The Ages*, 2000.

Fairbairn, Patrick. *Prophecy*, 1976.

Fisher, C H. *The Pre-Tribulation Rapture*, 2001.

Foster, Ivan. *Shadow Of The Antichrist*, 1996.

Frost, Henry W. *Matthew Twenty-four And The Revelation*, 1924.

Fruchtenbaum, Arnold G. *The Footsteps Of The Messiah*.

Gentry, Kenneth L. *The Beast Of Revelation*, 1989.

——————. *House Divided: The Break-up of Dispensational Theology*, 1997.

Glasson, T. Francis. *The Second Advent*, 1947.

——————. *His Appearing & His Kingdom*, 1953.

Gleason, R.W. *The World To Come*, 1958.

Goodspeed, Calvin. *Messiah's Second Advent*, 1900.

Gordon, A.J. *Behold He Cometh*, 1889.

Graham, Billy. *Approaching Hoofbeats—The Four Horsemen Of The Apocalypse*, 1983.

——————. *Till Armageddon*, 1981.

Gundry, Robert. *The Church And The Tribulation*, 1973.

——————. *First the Antichrist*, 1997.

Hagee, John. *From Daniel To Doomsday*, 1999.

Hayford, Jack E. *Quake*, 1999.

Hendriksen, William. *More than Conquerors*, 1940.

Hitchcock, Mark. *101 Answers To The Most Asked Questions*

About End Times, 2001.

Hobbs, Herschel H. *The Cosmic Drama—An Exposition of the Revelation*, 1971.

Hodges, Jesse Wilson. *Christ's Kingdom and Coming*, 1957.

Hoekema, Anthony. *The Bible And The Future*, 1979.

Houghton, Thomas. *The Faith And The Hope Of The Future*, 1925.

Hughes, Phillip E. *Interpreting Prophecy*, 1976.

Hunt, David. *Peace Prosperity And The Coming Holocaust*, 1983.

Ice, Thomas & Demy T. *The Truth About The Rapture*, 1996.

Jeremiah, David. *Escape The Coming Night*, 1990.

Jones, Russell Bradley. *The Great Tribulation*, 1980.

——————. *The Latter Days*, 1961.

Kellogg, Samuel. *The Jews Or Prediction And Fulfillment*, 1887.

Kennedy, H.A.A. *St Paul's Conceptions Of The Last Things*, 1905.

Kern, Lynn R. *Jesus Is Coming! But When?* 1999.

Kik, J. Marcellus. An *Eschatology Of Victory*, 1971.

Kimball, William R. *What the Bible Says About the Great Tribulation*, 1983.

Kromminga, D.H. *The Millennium*, 1948.

Kuenzi, Vernon L. *Restoring the Vision of the End-times Church*, 2001.

Ladd, George Eldon. *The Blessed Hope*, 1956.

——————. *Critical Questions About The Kingdom Of God*, 1952.

——————. *The Gospel of the Kingdom*, 1959.

——————. *The Presence Of The Future*, 1974.

——————. *Revelation*, 1972.

————————. *The Last Things*, 1978.

LaHaye, Tim. *Rapture (Under Attack)*, 1998.

————————. *Are We Living in the End Times?*

————————. *Revelation,* 1973.

————————. *Revelation Unveiled*, 1999.

LaHaye, T., Jenkins, J. *Left Behind*, 1995.

Lalonde, Peter & Patti. *Left Behind,* 1995.

Larkin, Clarence. *The Book Of Daniel*, 1929.

Lenski, R.C.H. *Interpretation Of St. John's Revelation*, 1943.

Levitt, Zola. *The Signs Of The End*, 1978.

————————. *The Second Coming*, 1979.

Liddon, H. P. *Advent In St. Paul's*, 1889.

Lightner, Robert. *Last Days Handbook*, 1997.

Lilje, Hanns. *the Last book of the Bible*, 1950

Lindsey, Hal. *Late Great Planet Earth*—Collection, 1970

Lovett, C. S. *Latest Word On The Last Days*, 1980.

Lowe, William G. *Even So, Come Lord Jesus*, 1973.

MacPherson, David. *The Three Rs*, 1998.

————————. *The Rapture Plot*, 2000.

MacPherson, Ian. *Dial The Future*, 1975.

MacPherson, Norman S. *Tell It Like It Will Be*, 1970

Martin, Ralph. *Is Jesus Coming Soon?—A Catholic Perspective*, 1983.

Mauro, Philip. *Things Which Soon Must Come To Pass*, 1974.

McConkey, James H. *The End Of The Age*, 1942.

————————. *The Book Of Revelation*, 1921.

Michaels, Ramsey. *Interpreting the Book of Revelation*, 1992.

Milligan, William. *Revelation, Discussion On The Apocalypse*, 1893.

Moody, Dale. *The Word Of Truth*, 1981.

Moody, Dwight L. *The Second Coming Of Christ*.

Morgan, G. Campbell. *The Parables Of The Kingdom*, 1998.

──────. *Behold He Cometh*, 1976.

Morris, Leon *Revelation of St. John*, 1969.

Montgommery, Don. *Rapture—Post Tribulation And Pre Wrath*, 1995.

Nee, Watchman. *Come, Lord Jesus*, 1976.

Newton, B.W. *The Coming Of The Lord*, 1869.

Newton, Sir Isaac. *Observations Upon the Prophecies Of Daniel & Revelation*, 1733.

Nigrio, H.L. *Before God's Wrath*, 2000.

Payne, Barton J. *Encyclopedia of Biblical Prophecy*, 1973.

Peake, Arthur S. *The Revelation Of John*, 1919.

Pentecost, Dwight J. *Things To Come*, 1958.

Phillips, John B. *Exploring The Future*, 1927.

Pieters, Albertus. *The Facts And Mysteries Of The Christian Faith*, 1952.

Pink, Arthur W. *The Antichrist*, 1923.

──────. *The Prophetic Parables Of Matthew 13*, 1918.

──────. *The Redeemer's Return*, 1918.

Pollock, A.J. *Things Which Shortly Must Come To Pass*, 1918.

Poole-Conner, E J. *The Coming Of The Son of Man*, 1947.

Ramsey, William. *Zion's Glad Morning*, 1990.

Reese, Alexander. *The Approaching Advent of Christ*, 1975.

Reinhold, Roy A. *The Day of the Lord: Prophecy* Revealed, 1986.

Rimmer, Harry. *Palestine—the Coming Storm Center*, 1940.

Robertson, Pat. *The Secret Kingdom*, 1982.

Robinson, John A.T. *Jesus And His Coming*, 1957.

Rose, George L. *Tribulation Till Translation—Compendium of Prophecy*, 1943.

Rosenthal & Howard. *The Feasts Of The Lord—God's Prophetic Calendar*, 1997.

Rosenthal, Marvin. *The Pre-Wrath Rapture Of The Church*, 1999.

Rowlands, W J. *Our Lord Cometh*, 1930.

Ryle, J.C. *Warnings To The Churches*, 1967.

Scofield, C.I. *What Do The Prophets Say?* 1916.

Scott, C. Anderson. *The Book of the Revelation*, 1922.

Scruby, John B. *The Great Tribulation, The Church's Supreme Test*, 1933.

Seraiah, C Jonathin. *The End Of All Things*, 1999.

Showers, Renald. *Maranatha Our Lord, Come!* 1995.

Simpson, A.B. *The Christ in the Bible—Thessalonians to Revelation*, 1973.

Skolfield, Ellis H. *SOZO Survival Guide For A Remnant Church*, 1995.

Smith, Oswald J. *Prophesy—What Lies Ahead?* 1965

————. *World Problems In The Light of Prophecy*.

Smith, Uriah. *Daniel And The Revelation*, 1944

Snowden, James H. *The Coming Of The Lord*, 1922

Spicer, W.A. *Our Day In The Light of Prophecy*, 1917

Sproul, R.C. *The Last Days According To Jesus*, 1998.

Spurgeon, Charles. *The Second Coming*, 1996.

Summers, Ray. *Worthy is the Lamb*, 1951.

————. *The Life Beyond*, 1959.

Sutton, Hilton. *Rapture*, 1997.

————. *The Book of Revelation Revealed*, 1998.

Swete, Henry Barclay. *The Life Of The World To Come*, 1917.

——————. *The Apocalypse Of St. John*, 1909.

Tenney, Merrill C. *Interpreting Revelation*, 1957.

Thigpen, Paul. *The Rapture Trap*, 2001.

Toms, Alan. *I Will Come Again*, 1963.

Tregelles, S. P. *The Man Of Sin*.

——————. *The Hope Of Christ's Second Coming*, 1864

——————. *Remarks On The Prophetic Visions In The Book Of Daniel*, 1965.

VanGemeren, William. *Prophetic Word*, 1990.

Van Impe, Jack. *The Great Escape, Preparing for the Rapture*, 1998.

VanKampen, Robert. *The Rapture Question Answered*, 1997.

Vos, Geerhardus. *The Pauline Eschatology*, 1930.

——————. *Teachings of Jesus—The Kingdom of God and the Church*, 1930.

Waldron, Samuel E. *The End Times Made Simple*.

Walvoord, John. *Armageddon, Oil And The Middle East*, 1974.

——————. *End Times*, 1998.

——————. *Major Bible Prophecies*, 1994.

——————. *The Revelation of Jesus Christ*, 1966.

——————. *The Rapture Question*, 1957.

West, Nathaniel. *The Thousand Years*, 1889.

Westcott, Brooke Foss. *The Gospel Of The Resurrection*, 1913.

Wilkerson, David. *Jesus Christ Solid Rock—The Return of Christ*, 1972.

——————. *America's Last Call*.

Winklhofer, Alois. *The Coming of His Kingdom*, 1963.

Woodrow, Ralph. *Great Prophecies Of The Bible*, 1971.

——————. *The Secret Rapture Is It Scriptural?* 1989.

Chapter 1—Correctly Handling the Word of Truth

[1] Webster's New World Dictionary—Third College Edition—1989.

Chapter 2—According to the Lord's Own Word

[1] Thayer's Greek-English Lexicon by Joseph H, Thayer—*parousia,* #3952.

[2] Strong's Hebrew and Greek Dictionaries, *ethnos* G1484.

[3] Luke 21:11.

[4] Strong's Hebrew and Greek Dictionary—*megus,* G3173.

[5] Strong's Hebrew and Greek Dictionary—*thlipsis,* G2347.

[6] Strong's Hebrew and Greek Dictionary—*eklektos,* G1588.

[7] Strong's Concordance with Hebrew and Greek Dictionaries—*airo,* G142.

[8] Strong's ibid—*paralambano,* G3880.

Chapter 3—Spoken of Through the Prophet Daniel

[1] Strong's Concordance transliterated Hebrew and Greek—*shabuwa,* H7620.

2 Sir Robert Anderson, The Coming Prince, 1895—Kregel Classics 1957.

3 Strong's Concordance transliterated Hebrew and Greek—*mashiyach*, H4899.

4 Strong's Concordance transliterated Hebrew and Greek—*nagiyd*, H5057.

5 Sir Robert Anderson, The Coming Prince, 1895—Kregel Classics 1957.

6 Strong's Concordance transliterated Hebrew and Greek—*karath*: H3772.

7 Flavius Josephus, The complete Works, Book 5.

8 Flavius, Book 6.9.3.

9 Strong's Concordance transliterated Hebrew and Greek—*amad* H5975.

Chapter 4—Listen, I Tell You a Mystery

1 Barclay-Newman Greek Dictionary—*musterion,* #3466.

2 *Thayer's Greek-English Lexicon of the New Testament,* May 2000—*eschatos,* #2078.

Chapter 5—Brothers, We do Not Want You to Be Ignorant

1 Strong's Concordance with Hebrew and Greek Dictionaries—*epiphaneia,* G2015.

2 Strong's Concordance with Hebrew and Greek Dictionaries, *apokalupsis* G605.

3 John F. Walvoord, *End Times,* Word Publishing, 1998, page 21.

4 *Vocabulary of the Greek Testament* by J. H. Moulton and G. Milligan, Hendrickson Publishers 1997—*parousia,* #3952.

5 *Vocabulary of the Greek Testament* by J. H. Moulton and G. Milligan, Hendrickson Publishers 1997—*apantesis,* #529.

6 Revelation 16.

[7] *The New Scofield Study Bible* (NIV), Oxford Publishers, 1998.

Chapter 6—Don't Let Anyone Deceive You in Any Way

[1] *Thayer's Greek-English Lexicon of the New Testament—apostasia*, #646.

[2] *Webster's New World Dictionary*—Third College Edition.

Chapter 8—Revelation of Jesus Christ

[1] *Strong's Concordance with Hebrew and Greek Dictionaries—tereo*, G5083

[2] *Thayer's Greek-English Lexicon of the New Testament* by Joseph H. Thayer, Hendrickson Publishers—*tereo*, #5083.

[3] *Strong's Concordance with Hebrew and Greek Dictionaries—ek*, G1537.

[4] Sir Isaac Newton, *Observations Upon The Prophecies of Daniel, And The Apocalypse of St. John*, 1733—page 251.

[5] *Strong's Concordance with Hebrew and Greek Dictionaries—sepher*, H1697.

[6] Strong's ibid—*biblos, G976.*

[7] Strong's ibid—*dabar, H1696.*

Chapter 10—You Have Heard It Said

[1] Ages Digital Library—The Master Christian Library—Version 8.

[2] *Ibid.*

[3] *Ibid.*

[4] *Ibid.*

[5] *Ibid.*

[6] *Ibid.*

[7] *Ibid.*

[8] *Ibid.*

[9] *Ibid.*

[10] *Ibid.*

[11] *Ibid.*

[12] *Ibid.*

[13] *Ibid.*

[14] *Ibid.*